BBC MUSIC GUIDES

COUPERIN

D1536777

BBC MUSIC GUIDES

Couperin

DAVID TUNLEY

BRITISH BROADCASTING CORPORATION

Published by the
British Broadcasting Corporation
35 Marylebone High Street
London W1M 4AA

ISBN 0 563 17851 5

First published 1982

Filmset in Great Britain by
August Filmsetting, Warrington, Cheshire
Printed in England by Hollen Street Press, Slough, Berks

Contents

To Gillian Weir

Introduction

Like more than one artist, François Couperin has suffered from being 'typecast' in popular imagination; in his case as a composer of elegant trifles written for a sophisticated, yet frivolous, audience. His cause has not been helped by some historians (particularly those outside France) who, from the time of Charles Burney onwards, seem to have been remarkably ignorant of the full extent of Couperin's music and out of sympathy with what they do know. In his famous *A General History of Music*, which was published towards the end of Couperin's century, Burney characterised the French composer's music as being 'so crouded and deformed by beats, trills, and shakes, that no plain note was left to enable the hearer of them to judge whether the tone of the instrument on which they were played was good or bad'. The same kind of remark came from Bach's first biographer, Johann Nicolaus Forkel, who admitted that, while Bach held Couperin's harpsichord pieces in very high esteem, the German master 'considered them as too affected in their frequent use of graces, which goes so far that scarcely a note is free from embellishment'. Whether this was the opinion of Bach or of Forkel (formed long after Bach's death) we shall never know, but the fact is that not only did the former composer transcribe the Rondeau from Couperin's sixth *Ordre* of harpsichord pieces for Anna Magdalena, but also that the aria which forms the theme of the Goldberg Variations is as lavishly ornamented as anything found in the French school. A later historian, Hubert Parry, in an influential book *The Evolution of the Art of Music* (described by H. C. Colles as 'one of the foundations of English musical literature', and in wide circulation until well after the Second World War) said of Couperin that he was 'evidently a man of considerable musical gifts of a high order who sacrificed more dignified lines of art in concession to French popular taste for ballet tunes'. Fortunately the composer was to find an eloquent champion in Wilfrid Mellers, whose *François Couperin and the French Classical Tradition* (1950) remains the one major study in English. Couperin's genius is recognised, of course, in James Anthony's *French Baroque Music* (revised edition, 1978) which provides essential reading for anyone interested in this wide and fascinating subject.

Perhaps it is not surprising that Burney, Forkel and Parry – to mention just these three – were out of sympathy with what they knew of Couperin's music, for they were as much products of their own times as Couperin and his music were of his. The elegantly polite manners of the courtly circles in which Couperin worked were not those of the more prosaic and middle-class environment of Burney and Forkel, any more than they were of Parry who moreover, as a late nineteenth-century musician and historian, was so blinded by the genius of Beethoven that he could see little beyond him, and judged almost everything by the yardstick of the German symphonic school. Not that we in the twentieth century are any closer to the manners of the *grand siècle*! But whatever the shortcomings of our times may be, we have at least acquired the capacity to judge the arts of earlier periods on their own terms and not impose upon them quite irrelevant standards of judgement.

Yet much French music of the seventeenth and eighteenth centuries still presents something of an enigma to many listeners who are baffled when some of the procedures or landmarks familiar in Italian and German baroque music seem to be missing from it. Much of this music, too, looks unpromising on paper or when tried over on the piano – often seemingly so simple in relation to the complexities of the music of, say, J. S. Bach. More perhaps than any other, French music of this period depends upon stylish performance to reveal its elusive secrets; if the listener is attuned to the style then the rewards from such a performance can be richly satisfying.

The present book, therefore, is not a series of programme notes or concert annotations, but a study of Couperin's style seen through aspects of specific works, and viewed in the wide perspective of French and Italian (and hence, German) musical practices during the seventeenth and early eighteenth centuries. Couperin's pieces will then speak for themselves.

During the preparation of this book I have been helped immeasurably and in different ways – some small, some large but all vital – by a number of people: Dr Meredith Little (Ellis) of Tucson, Arizona, and Mr Tom Green in Paris, while at home Miss Jennifer Wildy, Librarian of the Wigmore Music Library of the University of Western Australia, has given me her customary unstinted help. For the translation and interpretation of the relevant sections of the *Caeremonial Pariense* (1668) I am indebted to Fathers John Harte and Christopher Willcock; also to Dr Beverley Ormerod and Mr Brian Willis for helping translate some of the problematic passages in Couperin's texts and prefaces. Mrs Margaret Seares has read through the entire typescript and I owe much to her keen eye and critical judgement. The description of baroque dances (Appendix C) was compiled by Miss Margaret Mullins whose scholarly and practical knowledge of this area, together with the performances given under her direction by the University of Western Australia Baroque Dance Ensemble, has helped many of us to understand more fully the inseparable union between French music and dance in those days. It is hoped something of this is conveyed in the present book. To Miss Gillian Weir, to whom this book is dedicated, I owe a similar debt of gratitude for, during her periods as Musician-in-residence at the Department of Music in the University of Western Australia, her inspired playing of Couperin's organ and harpsichord music so illuminated the composer's keyboard style as to give me confidence to write about it. And finally, my deep thanks to my wife, Paula, who as always has smoothed the way to make the writing possible.

Department of Music,
University of Western Australia.

Couperin and his Times

The history of European music is essentially the history of changing styles. This becomes strikingly evident with the development of polyphony or part-writing which, as a uniquely European phenomenon, coincided with a new phase of Western civilisation in the eleventh and twelfth centuries; and from that time onwards European music has mirrored the restlessness of the European mind in its seemingly endless search for innovation and change. In a very real sense, this music is characteristically always in a state of transition.

The emergence, growth and decay of a style is a familiar enough pattern to those who have studied the various historical periods of music: medieval, renaissance, baroque, classical, romantic. In this pattern, while the rate of change may vary, the forward thrust of development is ever-present. The earlier phase in the development of a style is usually marked by a quickened pulse which slackens as the style matures and the forms are consolidated. Yet strangely, in the early and middle years of the seventeenth century this momentum apparently lost so much force in French music that the art seems to have settled into a long period of calm repose; and this was at the very time when Italian music was being swiftly borne by the powerful surge of that movement now usually described as the Baroque. The tranquil waters were deceptive. There were currents that carried French music into new parts, but they were more like little eddies, soon lost in the slow drift; then, towards the end of the century, the Italian flood broke its banks and washed into the music of France. One of the composers to feel and respond to the new force was the young François Couperin.

Born in 1668, François was the son of Charles Couperin, first of the family dynasty of organists at St Gervais in Paris. At that time there was still no sign of the changes which were to come over French music; these were still two decades away. The precocious musician absorbed the style around him – especially that of church music – with such spontaneity that his first published compositions (the two organ masses of 1690) are also among his indisputable masterpieces. Yet before the century was over, François Couperin was at the head of a movement which, from its encounter with Italian music, was to transform the French classical tradition he had inherited.

As far as vocal music was concerned, the most popular form in France during the first half of the seventeenth century was the *air de cour*. The name, as well as the style, had its origins in the late sixteenth century, and musical traits from these closing years of the Renaissance were to persist in France for many decades. The *air de cour* was a strophic song for several voices, or for solo voice with lute accompaniment, the two versions often existing side by side. As the new century wore on, the name became retracted simply to *air* – a loose, generic term which covered different categories of song, like *air sérieux, air à boire, air à danser, air tendre*. In the second half of the seventeenth century the solo form and duet were more extensively cultivated than the part-song. Couperin was to leave some agreeable examples.

The melodic style of all these seventeenth-century French songs was extremely simple. Just as Renaissance composers in France had moulded their melodies in suave contours and shapely phrases, so too did the next generation of song composers in that country do the same. One can take a group of French lute airs from the late Renaissance and find a striking similarity between these and many others written up to at least 1680.

The solo song had also been extensively cultivated in Italy from the early years of the seventeenth century. There, however, it had been one of the vehicles to carry the new fervent and declamatory style which heralded the Baroque era. In Italy lute accompaniment soon gave way to that provided by harpsichord and cello, this combination giving fuller rein to the harmonic intensity and richness characteristic of the new style. In France, on the other hand, the lute (or more correctly the *théorbe*) retained its position as the favoured instrument for accompaniment. As late as 1668 the composer and teacher Bénigne de Bacilly could claim that the *théorbe* or bass lute was far superior to the harpsichord when accompanying, as it did not obscure the voice.[1] The French air did not express the passionate intensity or display the bravura of the Italian aria. Quite the reverse. And what virtuosity there was lay in the subtle, delicate yet complex art of melodic decoration. This was known as *diminutions* or *doubles*, and we encounter it in one of Couperin's airs as well

[1] Bénigne de Bacilly, *Remarques curieuses sur l'art de bien chanter* (Paris, 1668), pp. 17–18. An English translation by Austin B. Caswell is published under the title *A Commentary upon the Art of Proper Singing* (New York, 1968).

as in some of his harpsichord music. Perhaps only in the *récits* of Pierre Guédron (1564–1621) can we find any influence of Italian monody – and this not to any marked degree. For the most part the French air is pervaded by a gentle languor or by the graceful rhythms of the dance. Only the drinking songs (*airs à boire*) caught a more energetic mood or enjoyed a hearty text. None, however, had much in common – either in spirit or technique – with the Italian baroque aria.

Indeed, the term 'baroque' seems scarcely applicable to French music until well on in the second half of the century, and then merely in part. Even the one element of the baroque era which seems to link its earlier to its latest exemplars is missing in French music until 1652. This is the so-called figured-bass continuo, whereby the keyboard player or lutenist who was accompanying a soloist or ensemble built up his harmonies by following a series of numerals (which indicated the chords) written below the notes in the bass. For some historians the existence of this system throughout the seventeenth and eighteenth centuries provides the only argument for placing Monteverdi with Bach under the canopy of the term 'baroque'. In France its use can be traced back to Du Mont's *Cantica Sacra* in the middle of the century, but it was not necessarily widely practised in that country. It was not, for example, until after 1672 that any of the airs in Ballard's great collection entitled *Airs de différents autheurs à deux parties* (1658–94) began to be issued with a figured-bass accompaniment either for lute or harpsichord. Whereas in Italy the harpsichord was increasingly supported by the cello, in France it was that noble old instrument from renaissance times which filled this role: the bass viol.

The *basse de viole*, in fact, retained a special place in French music until well into the eighteenth century. In Italy and Germany it was largely a curiosity by this time, although Bach's sixth Brandenburg Concerto shows that it was by no means extinct. Particularly through the virtuosity of performer–composers such as Saint-Colombe, Marin Marais, Jean Rousseau and others, the tradition of solo bass viol playing developed to a very high level in France and lasted well into the eighteenth century when Couperin composed two splendid, and technically very demanding, suites for the instrument towards the end of his life.

These suites, like most works bearing the title, were largely made up of dance movements; and it is the dance which constitutes

France's most important contribution to music of the seventeenth century. These dances – her most exportable musical commodity – found their way into all countries of Europe, and the forms inspired some of the finest music outside France during the baroque period. With the notable exception of the sarabande and the passacaille from Spain, the chaconne from Mexico, the allemande from Germany and the gigue from England, most of the dances were native to France, having originated in the provinces and been brought to the court ballroom where they were refined and stylised. As France gained leadership over Italy in cultivating the manners of polite society, so French court dance became an essential accomplishment for the nobility, the lead being given by the King himself. Louis XIV was an excellent dancer, and it has been reported that in his youth he assiduously practised the courante for some hours a day.[1] Although it formed the basis of theatrical dance, which included leaps and much agility, social dance was by contrast always elegant and smooth in execution, its movements an extension of courtly deportment, its steps forming a counterpoint against the rhythm of the music. Indisputably, the dance in all its manifestations was the most important form of music in France. So influential was it in that country that it could truly be said that music there aspired to the condition of the dance. No clearer indication of its influence could be found than in French music for the harpsichord.

The French school of harpsichord playing is generally considered to have been founded by Jacques de Chambonnières (*c.* 1602–72) who was court player to Louis XIII. He followed the lead given by the lutenists of his day who, instead of playing in a strictly polyphonic style, gave the impression of an interplay of individual lines in a technique known as *style brisé* (or 'broken texture'). To this Chambonnières and his school added the greater range of colour and sonority of the keyboard and developed a style which became the model for generations of harpsichord composers in France.[2] For many people this kind of music seems to contain the quintes-

[1] Pierre Rameau, *Le Maître à danser* (Paris, 1725), p. 110. See also Wendy Hilton, 'A Dance for Kings: the Seventeenth-century French Courante', *Early Music* (OUP), vol. 5, no. 2, April 1977.

[2] For a famous description of Chambonnière's style of playing and that of some of his contemporaries see *Lettre de Mr. Le Gallois a Mlle. Regnault* (Paris, 1680) which has been translated and annotated by David Fuller in 'French harpsichord playing in the seventeenth century', *Early Music* (OUP), vol. 4, no. 1, January 1976.

sence of French music of that period, especially because of its rich and sophisticated ornamentation. For his harpsichord pieces, Chambonnières and those who followed him – D'Anglebert, Louis Couperin, La Barre and many others – found in the dance an ideal model. The stately allemande and noble sarabande provided the serious moments, the bourrée and gigue the gayer ones. In the French courante lay the possibilities for exploiting rhythmic suppleness, and all these dances, together with the minuet, gavotte, passepied, rigaudon and others found their way into the instrumental music of all countries. It is also worth noting that the passacaglia (passacaille) and chaconne, which were included in instrumental suites in all countries, were still being danced in France until the early eighteenth century even though they appear to have lost all association with the ballroom elsewhere. In seventeenth-century France the only movements of the keyboard suite completely independent of the dance were the 'unmeasured' preludes of D'Anglebert and Louis Couperin; these provided the performer with the pitch only of the notes, leaving their rhythmic interpretation to his improvisatory skill. With these models before him it is surprising that François Couperin left no examples of the form. He did however compose some measured preludes which he included in his pedagogical work *L'Art de toucher le clavecin*.

If the influence of the dance was strongly exerted in harpsichord music and in some songs, it was of course at the very heart of those royal entertainments, the *ballets de cour*. The French counterpart of the English masque and Italian *mascherata*, the *ballet de cour* embraced dancing, dialogue and singing in allegorical homage to the king. With the appearance of the Italian-born Lully the *ballet de cour* entered a new phase, and in the hands of the same composer was later to be transformed into French opera (*tragédie lyrique*) which, unlike that of Italy, featured chorus, ballet and spectacle, all integral features of the earlier form. Although Couperin wrote no operas, neither he nor any French composer of that time could escape the influence of *tragédie lyrique* or ignore the presence of its originator, Jean-Baptiste Lully (1632–87), a composer to whom Couperin paid deep tribute in his orchestral suite entitled *L'Apothéose composé à la mémoire de l'incomparable Monsieur de Lully* (1725).

It is no mere artistic licence to place Lully, master of the heroic gesture, alongside those other great figures of French classicism: Corneille, Racine, Le Nôtre, Poussin, Le Brun. When permitted to form his own orchestra at court, called *Les petits violons* (in contrast to *Les vingt-quatre violons du Roy*), he did away with any improvised ornamentation, replacing it with a plainer manner of performance marked by a crisp precision attained through a style of bowing which was new to orchestral playing. This became famous throughout Europe. As well as composing dances and airs for his ballets and operas, Lully moulded a style of vocal writing that became the pride of France although hardly the envy of Italy. It was a style in which declamation merged imperceptibly into lyricism, baffling the Italians who preferred to keep these two elements quite separate in recitatives and arias.

Although the Italians did not appreciate Lully's vocal style, they (and the Germans) fully admired and imitated one feature of his operas and ballets: the *ouverture*. This was devised by Lully as a great fanfare to his courtly entertainments, commencing as it always did with majestic dotted rhythms giving way eventually to a more lively section in fugal style, and often concluding with dance movements. It was a musical form that found great favour outside France in orchestral and keyboard music, while in the country of its origin the French 'overture' provided the only extended form of instrumental music until the later years of the seventeenth century.

It was only in church and keyboard music that Lully exerted no direct influence, and although he wrote some motets these follow the pattern already set by others, and certainly do not reach the level of those by his contemporary, Michel-Richard Delalande. His was not the world of the chapel and organ loft. By contrast, this was very much the world inhabited by the young Couperin who succeeded his father as organist at St Gervais in Paris. It is not surprising, then, that Couperin's output includes many very fine motets as well as the two masterly organ masses, a form which some French composers of the seventeenth century made peculiarly their own.

Air, dance, harpsichord suite, motet, organ mass, ballet, *tragédie lyrique*, all these with their forms and characteristic French expression were inherited by Couperin from the musical tradition of his own country. In all but those belonging to the dramatic genres he left enduring examples. Yet Couperin was also one of the first composers in France to take up the Italian style, which by this time was reaching full maturity in its own country.

When Couperin was seventeen, Archangelo Corelli (1653–1713) had just published his first book of trio sonatas for two violins and basso continuo. With these works the form of the trio sonata was firmly established. It was to the baroque era what the string quartet was to the classical period of the late eighteenth century, and like the later form the trio sonata was widely cultivated outside the country of its origin. Performer and composer, Corelli conceived his music in terms of his own instrument – the violin – and hence his sonatas make much use of rapidly repeated notes, wide skips and figures which return to an open string, all this resulting in themes which have great vitality and expansiveness in fast movements, and a rich lyricism indebted to the bel canto aria in the slow ones. This clearly recognisable 'sonata style' stood in sharp contrast to string writing in France, the style of which had been shaped by Lully's orchestral accompaniments to his ballets and operas. Like Italian opera, the Italian sonata style conquered Europe but made no immediate inroads into France, checked by that indifference to foreign music which she had shown throughout most of the century. The reasons for this indifference are harder to find in the earlier decades than in the later ones. At the beginning of the century there was certainly no ignorance of the new Italian currents, for the marriage of Maria de Medici to Henri IV of France in 1600 brought about many visits to Paris by Italian musicians, including the famous Caccini whose influential book *Le Nuove Musiche* (1602), has given its name to this formative period of the Baroque. In the middle years of the century indifference turned into hostility, at least as far as opera was concerned, although this was probably due more to political than purely musical reasons – the unpopular Cardinal Mazarin having engineered performances by Italian companies from motives *not* purely musical.

One of the reasons why monody (solo singing) and, later, opera had difficulty in taking root in France was undoubtedly the firm hold of the *ballet de cour*, its simple airs and graceful dances being quite alien to the spirit of the *nuove musiche*. Away from court circles, what centres of artistic activity there were in the first half of the century leaned more towards literary interests. This was especially so at the Hôtel du Rambouillet where Vincent Voiture (1597–1648) led the school of poets known as the *précieux*, and it is hard to avoid the conclusion that the spirit of this literary movement permeated French song throughout most of the century. Benigne de Bacilly, for example, takes pains in his *Remarques curieuses sur l'art de bien chanter* (1668) to show how certain verbal expressions acceptable in

Italian texts would be considered to be in bad taste in French ones.[1]

With the personal reign of Louis XIV, commencing in 1661, all the arts underwent a form of bureaucratic control unknown elsewhere, leading to a high degree of centralisation in the performance of music. With Versailles as the focal point, it is easy to see why in the second half of the century music remained aloof from foreign influence. The best French musicians sought appointment there, either in the *musique de chambre*, the *musique de la chapelle* or the *musique de l'écurie*. Some, like Couperin, worked part-time as court musicians. In his case he filled the posts of organist at St Gervais in Paris and, during the January quarter of each year, at the Royal Chapel. Like those of most musicians in the service of the King, his duties at court did not lie solely in one area. Although officially he was engaged to serve in the Royal Chapel, there were many occasions when he performed in the *musique de chambre*, and he was also harpsichord teacher to some of the royal children. Louis XIV had a genuine love of music and took an active interest in it throughout most of his long life. It was he, for example, who made the final choice when Couperin competed for the position of organist at the Royal Chapel. He also recognised that music was a powerful force in radiating the majesty of his person.[2] Thus, all prologues to dramatic entertainment at court extolled the virtues of the Sun King, and the music which accompanied these flattering words was appropriately noble and impersonal. The King's taste was the arbiter of musical fashion, and in his court musician, Lully, he found the man best able to satisfy it. As the King abhorred the unusual and bizarre, so Lully's music was couched in a language which avoided those striking modulations and dissonances to which many Italian composers were prone, moving instead in bland and simple, yet thoroughly effective, harmony. Seemingly the very embodiment of the French classical style in music, his operas exerted a profound influence over all musicians in that country, and it is difficult to cite another instance in which the music of one man summed up the style of a whole epoch. His personal influence went much further than the court when he was given complete control over all public performances of dramatic music in France, none of which could take place without his express permission. Only in the field of church music did his hand have no controlling power. In the realm

[1] Bacilly, *op. cit.*, p. 69.
[2] See Robert M. Isherwood, *Music in the Service of the King* (Ithaca, 1973).

of dramatic music his power was almost as absolute as that of the man who employed him. When Couperin was born, Lully had just created the *tragédie lyrique* and was entering the most brilliant phase of his career, ending only at his death in 1687. The king had nearly thirty years left during which time his musical tastes became increasingly insular. There seemed even less chance than before for Italian music to gain a foothold at Versailles.

Versailles, however, was not to maintain its hold over French artistic life for much longer. In the last two decades of the century the king was deeply troubled by political problems and personal bereavements, and these, together with the influence of the pious Mme de Maintenon whom he married after the death of the queen, distracted him from the pleasures of the court. With the decline of artistic activity at Versailles music began to be cultivated increasingly in Paris – in the salons of the wealthy and in the music-rooms of performers and composers. As the court became more insular, so Paris became more cosmopolitan. One of the results of this was the discovery and performance of Italian music, particularly those works of chamber music dimensions: the cantata and sonata, two forms which French composers had never cultivated. One of the seed-beds of Italianism in Paris was the household of the Duke of Orleans, future Regent of France, an avid music-lover and one devoted to music from Italy; but it is reported that when he wished to hear one of Corelli's sonatas played, there was no French violinist capable of playing them.[1] However, such a situation was soon to change.

The vogue for Italian music led at first to a spate of imitations by French composers. One French composer caught up in the wave of Italianism was the twenty-five-year-old François Couperin who, changing around the letters of his name, wrote several trio sonatas which he passed off as being written by an Italian composer, a deception which he revealed many years later when he published these works as the first movements of his collection of sonatas called *Les Nations*. (Unfortunately, he left no clue to his Italian *nom-de-plume*, but André Tessier has suggested the possibilities of 'Coperuni' or 'Pernucio'.[2]) As might be expected, Italian music was not received enthusiastically in all quarters, and controversy over the merits or shortcomings of one or the other national styles raged

[1] Michel Corrette, *Le Maître de clavecin pour l'accompagnement* (Paris, 1753).
[2] André Tessier, *Couperin* (Paris, 1926), p. 26.

18

for some years. To read the arguments and prejudices of the pamphleteers is to imagine that an inseparable gulf separated the two schools. Yet some composers, including Couperin, demonstrated through their music that French and Italian styles could be joined in a fruitful union. From this union sprang the French cantata, a form which found such favour that it was cultivated by almost all French composers active in the first half of the eighteenth century. Couperin is said to have composed some cantatas, but no examples have ever been found. The solo and trio sonata were also born from this union, the finest examples of the former coming from Jean-Marie Leclair, and of the latter from François Couperin. In their mature works the Italian techniques became wholly absorbed into the composers' personal styles. The bringing together of *le goût français* with *le goût italien* became a veritable artistic ideal for Couperin who declared (in the words of Apollo in *L'Apothéose de Lully*) that through it will be achieved 'the perfection of music'. At the very least it can be said that through this encounter of styles the French classical tradition in music was enriched and, in part, transformed, the grand manner of Lully giving way to music of more personal, intimate and vivacious expression which caught the spirit of the new century.

If less heroic, the new style was nevertheless, like the old, still an art of musical *gesture* rather than one of cogent argument such as is found, for example, in the music of J. S. Bach. Just as the enchanting canvases of Antoine Watteau reflected the moods and manners of an age in which society, less formal though no less polite than before, enjoyed the pleasures of the *fêtes galantes*, so too did the music of this same society acquire a seemingly easy and natural grace and a nuance of movement that we must try to recognise two and a half centuries later. It is unfortunate that the etiquette and deportment practised in eighteenth-century French society has been so mercilessly caricatured in comedies and operas as to give us the impression of affectation and foppishness; both were as frowned upon in those days as they are laughed at on stage today. In fact, gesture and bearing, studied and practised from the earliest years of childhood, produced a beauty and fluency of movement that we are much the poorer without. The very acts of walking, bowing, of holding a fan or removing a hat, of entering a room or sitting in a chair, the position of one arm in relation to the other, and these in relation to the rest of the body and head – all these movements and postures achieved a balletic grace as well as a nobility of manner gained through the rigorous discipline of courtly deportment. As we learn through the courtesy books and dance manuals of the time which have come down to us, the five basic 'positions' of social dance (which was to form the basis of nineteenth-century classical ballet) were also the basic 'positions' of deportment cultivated during the reign of Louis XIV. It is not the least surprising, therefore, that a society which developed physical movement to the level of an art, and which regarded the fine arts as a means of 'pleasing and touching' its audience (to borrow Racine's phrase) should have cultivated a style of music in which subtle and expressive 'gestures' were preferred to thematic argument. As we shall see in later chapters, such a style strongly influenced French melody and harmony, giving to them a characteristic complexion that even the union with Italian music could not disguise.

It may well have been this fascination with gesture and movement that led French musicians to linger frequently over the first of a pair of notes (making up for this by playing the second one more quickly). This imparted greater rhythmic vivacity and suppleness to an otherwise smooth flow of melody. The convention was known as *notes inégales* and, although also propounded by Caccini in his *Le Nuove Musiche*, it does not seem to have taken on in Italian music. Certainly in Couperin's day it was regarded as an essentially French practice. In a sense, it was a form of ornamentation applied spontaneously in performance – an embellishment of rhythm which, like those more familiar forms of embellishment, such as trills and mordents, contributed to that 'nuance of movement' referred to earlier. The Prelude of Couperin's first *Ordre* in the *Concerts royaux* (the opening of which is given at Ex. 19, p. 62) illustrates to perfection what has been said. The melody consists of three basic 'gestures' (and their variants) marked *a*, *b*, *c*, in the analysis, each of which is enlivened by the tiny movements of the melodic embellishments suggested by Couperin. (In this piece the performer may also wish to play the descending phrase at measure 7 in the rhythm of *notes inégales*, as the fancy takes him.)

Thus, one of the functions of ornamentation is to impart further suppleness of movement to the music. The rhythmic nuances gained by the musical gesture through sensitive ornamentation had their counterpart in theatrical dance, particularly in the dances choreographed by Guillaume-Louis Pécour, *maître de ballet* at the

Opéra from 1687 to 1729.[1] As in music, dance ornaments were known as *agrémens*, and they served to embellish basic steps, imparting (as in vocal and instrumental music) a high degree of virtuosity and brilliance to performance. But above all, the purpose of ornamentation in French music was to heighten the expressiveness already present in the poetry of gesture, whether this was in the dance or the music. Much ornamentation, particularly in vocal music, was left to the discretion of the performer, the composer being usually content to mark with a little cross those notes he wished to be embellished by singer or instrumentalist who, through training, experience and taste, would choose the appropriate ornament, ideally as a spontaneous act (see Exx. 4 to 9, pp. 34–43). On the other hand, for their harpsichord music, most composers (Couperin in particular) preferred to be more specific, indicating the various ornaments through shorthand signs placed near the notes. This matter is taken up on p. 77.

It will quite rightly be gathered from what has been said so far that ornamentation was an inseparable part of Couperin's expressive language. In the hands of the right performer it becomes dissolved into the flow of melody. Far from sounding as if it has been 'added' to the music, it seems to rise up from within, like a balletic movement held, extended or embellished by the dancer. Burney's complaint that Couperin's music was 'crouded and deformed by beats, trills and shakes' is less a criticism of the composer than an admission of his own inability to understand the style. It is important that we do not make the same mistake.

Nor should we imagine for a moment that Couperin's music is merely a mirror of what we tend, erroneously, to imagine was an artificially elegant – almost inhuman – society; music that reflected only the graceful movements of aristocratic deportment. It is true that good breeding demanded total observance of what was called *complaisance* – a quality once described by Shirley Wynne as an eighteenth-century 'cool': 'the demeanour which in all appearances was one of controlled vitality'.[2] Yet Couperin must have felt as deeply as any man, and in his music how much he suggests by a single, penetrating glance. 'Controlled vitality' is indeed the perfect

[1] See Margaret Mullins, 'Music and Dance in the French Baroque', *Studies in Music* (University of Western Australia), no. 12, 1978.

[2] Shirley Wynne, 'Complaisance, an Eighteenth-Century Cool', *Dance Scope* (American Dance Guild), vol. 5, no. 1, 1970.

description of his music. As we shall see, his output, though largely couched in French terms, covers a wide range of musical experience through the amalgam of French and Italian styles. His early trio sonatas, as we might expect when the composer sought to emulate Corelli, catch much of the warmth and brilliance of the Italian sonata style, while in his harpsichord pieces, the Italian elements are more subtly woven into the music. Yet even here we find a wealth of variety, from dances which spring from the pure classical tradition to works which, while unmistakably French, borrow some of the techniques of thematic development common to Italian and German music of the day.

Couperin is often linked with Rameau, as Bach is with Handel. Jean-Philippe Rameau, however, was twenty years younger than Couperin, and although he too was influenced by the Italian school, he was not part of that generation of composers who expanded and transformed the French classical tradition. His early career was largely concerned with his remarkable theoretical writings and with a few short compositions. His handful of cantatas were nearly all composed in the 1720s, by which time the form had reached its maturity in France. These, the most Italianate of his works, were somewhat in the nature of apprentice-pieces to his most enduring productions – his operas, all of which were composed after Couperin's final publication of 1730. Rameau's greatness lay in his operas, a genre which Couperin never touched, preferring instead the more intimate style afforded by chamber music and harpsichord. Together, however, their output covers almost the entire range of French baroque music upon which they placed the unmistakable marks of genius. Both men were also pedagogues: Rameau the theorist, Couperin the teacher. If the former's *Traité de l'Harmonie* (1722) was the most important attempt to codify the harmonic practice of his day, providing the basis for most textbook teaching of the subject for the next two hundred years, the latter's *L'Art de toucher le clavecin* (1716) remains one of the most informative sources about the techniques of French harpsichord performance.[1] It also contains some interesting reflections about teaching the

[1] An English translation by Margery Halford under the title *The Art of Playing the Harpsichord* is published by Aldred Publishing (Port Washington, N.Y., 1974), containing also the French text of the original two editions. See also Ralph Kirkpatrick, 'On re-reading Couperin's L'Art de toucher le clavecin', *Early Music* (OUP), vol. 4, no. 1, January 1976.

instrument to young children. So concerned was he over the
dangers of unsupervised practice that he recommended locking the
harpsichord between lessons so that (as he says) his young pupils
'will not ruin in a moment all that I have been trying to instil over
three quarters of an hour'. To emphasise the point he mentions that
he himself always pockets the key! Equally unorthodox was his
approach to the question of when his pupils should learn to read
music. He writes:

One should begin to show notation to children only after they have a good
number of pieces at their fingertips. It is almost impossible for the fingers
not to get out of shape and be incorrectly used if the pupils are reading from
the music, or for the ornaments not to be spoilt. Besides, memory is so
much better developed when one learns by heart.

Such a view as this anticipates by two hundred and fifty years one
present-day system of instrumental teaching developed in post-
war Japan, a parallel which has so far gone unnoticed, and which
provides further confirmation that in François Couperin we
encounter one of the liveliest musical minds of his century.

Not a great deal is known about Couperin's life. What facts there
are come from Titon du Tillet's account in *Le Parnasse françois*
(1743), a few archival documents and from the title-pages and
prefaces to the composer's published music. He was born on
10 December 1668 in Paris, and was only eleven when his father
died. But such was the young boy's precocity that the parish
council appointed him to succeed his father when he reached the
age of eighteen. Until then the post was to be filled by Michel-
Richard Delalande, and the boy's training to be placed in the hands
of Jacques Thomelin, organist at Saint Jacques-le-boucherie, who
was also one of the four organists at the Royal Chapel. It was
Thomelin's post at Versailles which Couperin won in 1693 following the death of his master. The next year he was also appointed
harpsichord teacher to the royal children. In addition to these
appointments he secured in 1717 the post of harpsichordist in the
musique de chambre which had been held by the then enfeebled Jean-
Baptiste D'Anglebert, son of the famous seventeenth-century
player and composer, a position which Couperin passed on to his
daughter Marguerite-Antoinette in 1730.

Couperin had married early, and of his three children only
Marguerite-Antoinette became a professional musician. The other
daughter joined a religious order, while his son apparently died in

infancy. François Couperin died on 12 September 1733 and was buried in the church of Saint Joseph, part of the parish of Saint Eustache. His post at Saint Gervais had been given in 1723 to his cousin Nicolas Couperin who in turn was to pass it on to later generations of the Couperin family, their reign at Saint Gervais coming to an end in 1826.

As for Couperin the man, we know through his own admission that he suffered from poor health during the latter part of his life. As a young man he had eagerly sought honours and titles. His first publication in 1692 describes the twenty-four-year-old composer as Sieur de Crouilly (the area from where his father came), and about 1702 he was made a Knight of Rome, and also received the Cross of the Knights of Latran which gave him the right to call himself Chevalier Couperin. Yet none of the portraits we have of him show any hint of arrogant bearing, and his many witty and playful pieces suggest a man of great charm and good humour.

Ten years after Couperin's death in 1733, the writer Titon du Tillet entered the composer's name in his *Le Parnasse françois*, a book commemorating France's illustrious men and women, particularly those in the arts. He described Couperin's harpsichord pieces as 'filled with excellent harmony and having a noble and gracious melody', also mentioning that they can be played on the violin or flute as well as on the harpsichord.[1] It is good to be reminded that Couperin was no 'purist' as far as instruments were concerned. The orchestral suite *L'Apothéose de Lully* can be played on two harpsichords; some of the harpsichord duets can be played as solos by leaving out the middle line; while almost all the *Concerts royaux* and *Nouveaux concerts* can be played by virtually any group of instruments (or harpsichord alone). All that he required was that performers should follow his ornamentation. Just as politeness and noble bearing were everyday acts in the cultivated circles of eighteenth-century French society, so Couperin's music was for everyday use. We do it no service by imagining otherwise, for beneath its elegant surface lies that robustness which usually accompanies the finest art.

[1] Titon du Tillet, *Le Parnasse françois* (Paris, 1732, Supplement 1743), p. 665.

Sacred Music

While the name of François Couperin is not immediately associated with sacred music it is appropriate for us to begin with this genre. Not only does it represent the major concentration of his activities as a composer in his youth and early maturity; his music for the church includes some of his finest, if least-known, pages. These are contained in the two organ masses of 1690 (his first published works) and in his *Leçons de ténèbres* of 1714 with which he concluded his output of sacred music.

THE TWO ORGAN MASSES

The *Messe pour les paroisses* and the *Messe pour les couvents* are both contained in Couperin's first publication, the *Pièces d'orgue* (1690). Publication is perhaps too strong a word for a volume of music in which only the title-page is printed, the music itself being written out by the hand of one of the copyists employed by the Parisian publisher Ballard, a not uncommon practice when the composer was unable to afford the cost of engraving. At that time Couperin was only twenty-two and virtually unknown as a composer. Whatever the number of copies issued by Ballard, one only has survived, and this was discovered in the early years of the twentieth century at the library of Carpentras in southern France. The two organ masses had been known to the late nineteenth century but only through some inferior manuscripts which Guilmant had used as the basis for his edition early this century. Now, of course, the works exist in an authentic version.

Before coming to the works themselves it is helpful to know something about the kind of instrument for which Couperin wrote. French organ building during the seventeenth century had developed along lines quite different from those in Germany.[1] Certainly there were superficial similarities: the *grand orgue* (or main manual) which was associated with a large number of pipes placed above the player's head corresponded to the *hauptwerk* of the Ger-

[1] See Fenner Douglass, *The Language of the Classical French Organ* (New Haven and London, 1969). For a concise and particularly helpful description see Lawrence Phelps, 'A Brief Look at the French Classical Organ, its Origins and German Counterpart' (article accompanying Gillian Weir's performance of Couperin's *Pièces d'Orgue* on *Argo* 4BBA 1011–2).

man instrument, while the *positif de dos* with its more intimate character (its pipes in a higher register than those of the *grand orgue*) was placed, like the *rückpositiv*, behind the player's back. But whereas German instruments developed considerable resources in other manuals, particularly the pedals, those in France relied largely upon the *grand orgue* and the *positif de dos*; even the pedals on seventeenth-century French organs were, in a sense, 'extras'. Thus most of the movements of Couperin's two masses can, with notable exceptions, be played without pedals. But above all, it was the tonal quality that distinguished French from German instruments. While German builders produced organs which featured transparent and bright sounds ideal for the polyphonic music being written by the seventeenth- and eighteenth-century German masters, French builders sought tonal variety and colour. They made much use of the *tierce*, a rank of pipes which sounded a note two octaves and a third above a stronger 'foundation' note, reinforcing the fifth harmonic, and imparting to registrations which required the *tierce* a sonority very characteristic of the French classical organ. This practice of artificially bringing into prominence a particular overtone gave rise to stops known as 'mutations' and these (which included the *nazard* and *larigot*) were richly exploited by French builders, providing tonal combinations distinctly different from German instruments. They also developed to perfection the more robust reed stops, two of which became indispensable: the *trompette* (on the *grand orgue* and pedal) and the *cromhorne* (on the *positif*). Another reed, the *voix humaine*, was also found on most large instruments, but curiously enough was missing from Couperin's instrument at Saint Gervais.

The carefully calculated relationships between groups of stops on the two essential manuals led to a standardisation of registration unknown in Germany. That known as the *plein jeu* (the most characteristic sound of the classical French organ) was the result of a combination of stops from both *grand orgue* and *positif*, producing a rich, brilliant and dynamic tone to which composers turned for strong, direct utterances, like the opening 'Kyrie' of the *Messe pour les couvents*. The registration known as the *Tierce en taille,* with its poignant tenor solo wreathed in a halo-like accompaniment, called out for music of noble eloquence. Indeed, in French organ music, sound and sentiment were related to a degree unknown elsewhere. So strong was this relationship that composers very often gave the registration as the title of a movement. As an example let us take the settings of the 'Gloria' in Couperin's two masses, the texts obviously exerting a strong influence over the registration in both works.

Text	Messe pour les paroisses	Messe pour les couvents
Et in terra pax	Plein jeu	Plein jeu
Benedicamus te	Petite fugue sur le Chromhorne	Petitte fugue sur le Chromhorne
Glorificamus te	Duo sur les Tierces	Duo sur les Tierces
Domine Deus, Rex caelestis, Deus Pater omnipotens	Dialogue sur les Trompettes, Clairon et Tierce du Grand Clavier et le Bourdon avec le Larigot du Positif	Basse de Trompette
Domine Deus, Agnus Dei, Filius Patris	Trio à 2 dessus de Chromhorne et la basse de Tierce	Chromhorne sur la Taille
Qui tollis peccata mundi, suscipe deprecationem nostram	Tierce en Taille	Dialogue sur la Voix humaine
Quoniam tu solus Sanctus	Dialogue sur la Voix humaine	Trio, les dessus sur la Tierce et la basse sur la Trompette
Tu solus Altissimus Jesu Christe	Dialogue en trio du Cornet et de la Tierce	Récit de Tierce
In gloria Dei Patris, Amen	Dialogue sur les Grands jeux	Dialogue sur les Grands jeux

Clearly, all registration depended upon the resources of each instrument, but nevertheless there existed a remarkably high degree of tonal standardisation in France during the seventeenth-century. Composer-performers such as Le Bègue gave suggestions in their publications about which stops to use for certain registrations (like the *plein jeu*), and because some organs of the period have now been restored we have a very good idea as to how works like the *Messe pour les paroisses* and *Messe pour les couvents* sounded in those days. (This is in striking contrast to what little we know about the registration of German baroque organ music.) Because Couperin's organ music was conceived in terms of the classical French organ, it goes without saying that it will sound almost unintelligible if played on a nineteenth-century romantic organ. Some of the *Messe pour les paroisses* looks rather dull on paper. Yet when played on an instrument that possesses a close approximation to the tonal resources of Couperin's, it achieves a haunting beauty through the combination of its musical thought and the sensual allure of the sound itself.

Although Couperin's two works are thoroughly enjoyable in purely musical terms, they were composed to serve a liturgical function. The so-called organ mass was an extension of the age-old custom of responsorial singing in which priest and choir alternated in the chanting of plainsong. With the development of polyphony the choral response was often couched in elaborate versions of the plainsong. In the organ masses the instrument took over the role of the choir, and by Couperin's time the alternation of plainsong and organ response had become a tradition of many years' standing, and regulated by procedures laid down by the Church in France. While these procedures or *cérémoniales* varied in detail from place to place, in general terms they were very similar.[1] As organist at St Gervais, Couperin was expected to follow the procedures relating to musical performance laid down in the *Caeremoniale Parisiense* drawn up in 1668 for the diocese of Paris. As this document has sometimes been misinterpreted, giving the impression that the organ mass was bound by many strict regulations even to the point of specific registrations, we reproduce relevant passages as an Appendix to this volume (see p. 94).

Far from being hampered by many restrictions, the organist or composer had merely to ensure that out of the twenty or so occasions when the organ alternated with choir or priests in their chanting of the ordinary of the mass, seven of these instrumental responses should use the plainsong chosen for that service. This had to occur at the first and last utterance of the words *Kyrie eleison*, at *et in terra pax*, *suscipe deprecationem nostram*, *in gloria Dei Patris*, *Amen*, at the first *Sanctus* and *Agnus Dei*. As far as registration was concerned, the organist was only required on certain occasions (*suscipe deprecationem, tu solus Altissimus Jesu Christe*, during Holy Communion, the elevation of the Host and Chalice and at 'the solemn verse of the sequence') to choose quiet stops 'so that greater devotion is created in the soul of the clerics and people'. The organ was to remain silent throughout the *Credo*.

It would seem that the *Caeremoniale Parisiense* may not have extended to closed establishments such as convents; certainly Couperin's *Messe pour les couvents* has no plainsong basis at all, being

[1] See Edward Higginbottom, 'French Classical Organ Music and the Liturgy', Proceedings of the Royal Musical Association, vols. 103, 1976–7.

freely composed throughout. Yet even his mass 'for parishes' which is based upon the chant *Cunctipotens Genitor Deus* does not fully observe the requirements of the *Caeremoniale*. The sixth organ response or couplet of the 'Gloria', for example, corresponds to the words *Qui tollis peccata mundi, suscipe deprecationem nostram* – one of the occasions when the plainsong phrase at these words was required to be sounded. Yet this movement is freely composed, with only the merest hint of the plainsong through the drooping phrase which steals throughout the movement; as noted earlier, Couperin's registration here (for *tierce en taille*) calls on one of the instrument's loveliest sounds. On all other occasions in his *Messe pour les paroisses* Couperin observes the requirements related to plainsong, either by sounding it in long notes (as in the first and last 'Kyrie', in the first 'Sanctus' where it is treated in canon between the two lower parts, and in the 'Agnus Dei' where it stands in strong relief to the four other voices which weave a flowing fugue around it) or by moulding its notes into a fugue-like subject as shown in Ex. 1 overleaf. The presence of the plainsong can be traced to other movements as well as those required by the *Caeremoniale*, as for example in the second *couplet* of the 'Kyrie'. Here the opening notes of the chant become a fugal theme in a manner similar to that shown in Ex. 1, or in the movement which follows it, where the same notes form the framework of a shapely melody given out on the sweet tones of the *cromhorne*:

Ex.2
Gregorian Melody

Ex.1 Messe pour les paroisses

Gregorian Melody (Transposed)

On at least one occasion, the second *couplet* of the 'Gloria', the organ takes up the musical phrase of the vocal response which *precedes* it, as though commenting on what has just passed, a situation, of course, which occurs only when the *Messe pour les paroisses* is performed in its liturgical context. For most listeners their experience of both works is more likely to be from a concert performance, and probably a recorded one at that – this at least having the likelihood of being played on an appropriate instrument.

Like many a work originally destined for the liturgy, Couperin's *Messe pour les paroisses* and *Messe pour les couvents* are both thoroughly satisfactory as concert works, each being in the nature of a suite of

twenty-one contrasting and, for the most part, fairly short movements. Both masses are as much concerned with matching the
colourful ceremony enacted below the organ-loft as with evoking a
devotional atmosphere. They bring together elements of the
majestic, the theatrical, the worldly – these being projected by organ
tones which seem to leap from the instrument – as well as the quietly
reflective. Those who are familiar with Purcell's dance-inspired
anthems will not be unduly disturbed by the urbanity of Couperin's
masses. Nevertheless some of the more severe polyphonic movements, such as the opening of the *Messe pour les paroisses*, may seem
very strange in their harmonies despite the allure they gain from the
tonal radiance of the *plein jeu*. The passage Ex. 3 overleaf is far re-
moved from the familiar harmonic procedures found in music from
the same period by Italian or German composers.

Harmonies such as these seem to belong more to the old viol
fantasias of late Renaissance times. As far as Couperin and his
generation of French organ composers are concerned, the source
of this style lay in the music of Jehan Titelouze (1563–1633), the
founder of the French organ school, whose works left a deep im-
print on those who followed him. The constant fluctuation between
major and minor versions of a chord produces a chromaticism very
different in its feel from that practised by contemporary Germans
and Italians. James Anthony's description of seventeenth-century
French harpsichord music as operating in a 'pre-tonal shadow zone'
is equally applicable here. He writes: 'It is both an irritant, to those
of us who unfortunately began life with a built-in tonal bias, and at
the same time a constant delight to have one's tonal compass totally
disoriented.'[1]

It is not only in some of his harmonies, of course, that Couperin
reveals his French musical inheritance: a melody such as that found
in the 'Elévation' of the *Messe pour les couvents* (a movement which
in this mass replaces the 'Benedictus' and fulfils the role of a motet)
is inconceivable in terms of the Italian baroque music of that day.
It unfolds in an almost improvisatory way. So dependent is it upon
both the registration of the *tierce en taille* and the loving hand of
a player who understands the style, that on paper (or at the piano) it
seems to make little sense. Given the right artist and instrument, this
music comes into its own.

[1] James R. Anthony, *French Baroque Music from Beaujoyeulx to Rameau*
(New York, Revised Edition, 1978), pp. 248–9.

Ex.3   Messe pour les couvents

We will not find the French classical tradition expressed in so pure a form again in Couperin's music, even though it shines strongly in the *Leçons de ténèbres*. In a sense then, the two organ masses were for Couperin a beginning and an end.

Like the two organ masses, Couperin's *Leçons de ténèbres* were composed for church use, although like the earlier works they can be fully appreciated away from their liturgical setting. They were written for the office of matins during Holy Week when the Lamentations of Jeremiah are sung or recited in their entirety over Maundy Thursday, Good Friday and Holy Saturday.

Although he published only the first three lessons Couperin clearly intended to complete the whole cycle, for two years later he claimed to be composing the remaining six. These were never published, nor has any trace of them been found, even though Couperin has described the overall plan of the cycle: the first two lessons for each day were to be for solo voice and continuo, the third for two voices and continuo. This is the scoring of the three lessons which have come down to us.

It appears that the composition of these Tenebrae pieces had been stimulated by the success of a setting he had made of lessons for the last day of Holy Week for an order of nuns some three years earlier. With these already behind him, it is even more puzzling that the cycle never appeared (or survived) in its entirety. More's the pity, for the settings of 1714 are not only amongst Couperin's finest inspirations, but are amongst the indisputable masterpieces of the baroque era.

The Lamentations of Jeremiah the Prophet consist of five 'elegies' mourning the destruction of Jerusalem. A feature of the original Hebrew poems was that they took the form of 'alphabet acrostics', each verse beginning with a characteristic Hebrew letter which, in some cases, led to setting out the entire Hebrew alphabet in order. When the poems were translated into Latin this scheme disappeared, but it became traditional to precede each Latin verse with the original Hebrew letter. Although meaningless in their new context, these vestigial traces of the original poetic form were incorporated into the Gregorian setting of the text, a practice also followed by many composers from early times to the present day. The settings of these letters thus form little 'preludes' to each, as we shall see in Couperin's setting of the Lamentations for the service of matins at Easter.

The first of the eight canonical hours, the office of matins is held at night, the gradual extinguishing of the candles during this office in the last three days of Holy Week leading to the name *tenebrae* (shadows). Couperin describes his *Leçons* as being written for Wednesday; in reality they form part of the observances for Maundy Thursday, Couperin's comment being explained by the fact that matins began just before midnight. The office of matins is divided into three parts called *nocturns*, each part consisting of three psalms and three lessons, each of which is followed by a responsory. During Tenebrae the three lessons of the first nocturn of each evening are devoted to the Lamentations of Jeremiah, the first nocturn of Maundy Thursday taking the first fourteen verses, framing them with *Incipit Lamentatione . . .* and *Jerusalem, convertere . . .* The text and translation of the Lamentations are set out in the liturgical context of the first nocturn for Tenebrae in Appendix B (see p. 95).

Couperin's *Leçons de ténèbres* are bound even more firmly to the liturgical framework by the composer's use of the traditional plain-song associated with the words. At the beginning of the work we see Couperin's mastery in translating the centuries-old chant into the language of his own day.

Ex.4   1st Leçon de ténèbres
Gregorian Setting (Transposed)

Because the text is so long the Gregorian setting is predominantly syllabic. Only at the Hebrew letters (sung always to the same melodic phrase) are there moments of respite from this style, and these very brief. It is precisely at these points that Couperin takes up the tiny melismas of the chant and extends them into long cantilenas of extraordinary beauty. As will be seen from the excerpts below, the half-dozen or so notes of the plainsong are merely the starting-point for Couperin, sometimes generating only the first few bars. Sometimes they are used in inversion. Whatever the technique employed by Couperin, there can be no doubt about the source of inspiration of these passages.

Ex.5
(a) (transposed)

(b) (original pitch)

(c) (original pitch, notes inverted)

Not all the Hebrew letters set by Couperin have this plainsong basis. The third *Leçon*, for example, has no relationship to any part of the chant, and in any case explores styles scarcely touched by the first two, as we shall see.

Like the organ mass, the lessons for Tenebrae attracted a number of French composers, who established the custom of extending the plainsong settings of the Hebrew letters. Marc-Antoine Charpentier, for example, had gone even further than Couperin in this regard, his setting of the Lamentations being one of the most remarkable and original compositions to come from seventeenth-century France, the intensity of expression probably unmatched in its day. So too do Couperin's three *Leçons* reach high points of musical intensity, but the style is less unrelenting than that of the earlier settings by Charpentier. Nevertheless Couperin's natural bent for the gay, the brilliant, the witty was put aside completely when composing these works for Passiontide – and this at a time when he had just published his first book of harpsichord pieces in which these features found ebullient expression. Again, many of the techniques he had developed in bringing together French and Italian styles, particularly in his instrumental ensemble music, found no outlet in the *Leçons de ténèbres* except in aspects of harmony. There are, for example, no passages quite like that quoted from the *Messe pour les couvents* at Ex. 3, although at the same time Couperin's harmonic language is distinctly different from his Italian and German contemporaries. What Italian elements there are seem to come from a very much earlier period – that of Monteverdi. (The third *Leçon* contains passages which have a remarkable affinity with some from Monteverdi's Vespers of 1610.) Like the two organ masses the three *Leçons de ténèbres* are works apart. Lacking the more familiar landmarks both of Couperin's music for the salon and court as well as the immediately accessible Italian baroque style, the sombre world of his Tenebrae settings may not be easy for some to enter.

In the two solo settings, i.e. the first and second *Leçons*, we find a considerable amount of vocal writing in a style very different from that of, say, Bach or Handel. As mentioned in the opening chapter there emerged in France during the seventeenth century a vocal style in which declamation and lyricism merged, elements which the Italians and Germans kept apart in the separate forms of recitative and aria. Indeed, those sections described by Couperin as *récitatif* in the *Leçons* are indistinguishable from the others, except that the former tend to commence with sustained chords in the accompaniment, these soon giving way to a moving bass. From then on any attempt to distinguish between *récitatif* and *air* is pointless.

The Italian bel canto aria developed traits which became characteristic of the mid and late Italian baroque style, and because of its pervasive influence in other countries, including England (through Handel and others), such traits have come to be regarded as bearing the hallmarks of the baroque musical style in general. They included a strong penchant for generating melodies from little rhythmic and melodic 'cells' or motives, a technique often involving what is usually called 'sequential development'. In this technique the motive is repeated on different degrees of the scale, often with some modification which does not, however, disguise its identity. A well-known aria like 'Ev'ry Valley' from *Messiah* is typical of the style.

Notwithstanding the fact that the Italian and German masters used these devices to great effect, there is a degree of predictability in this technique which helps the listener follow the course of the melody, and this, together with great emotional warmth and (often) a strong degree of bravura, imparted to the Italian style an immediate appeal which it still seems in no danger of losing. There is some sequential development in Couperin's *Leçons*, but it tends to be reserved for the *vocalises* at the Hebrew letters. These form only a small proportion of the music, however. What of those longer movements in which the technique plays a far less prominent role? What are we to make of a melodic style in which the familiar landmarks are so often missing, resulting in music where there seems to be little 'thematic' material to hold on to when listening?

The first thing we have to do is to cast off any preconceived ideas about the importance of 'thematic development' and 'thematic conciseness' in music generally (a hangover from the prominence given in histories of music to the classical symphony, one of the sources of which was the aria), and to recognise that there is a vast amount of music in which this plays no part at all. Instead, we have to develop an awareness of the beauty of melodic *shape* upon which at certain times and in certain schools the notion of thematicism has been *imposed*. In other words, we need to see beyond the familiar processes of baroque and classical periods to the wider, more universal concept of musical lyricism, embodied as much in the *ballati* of the fourteenth-century Landini as the twentieth-century Webern, in Indian *raga* music and Gregorian chant – as well as in the melodies of Bach, Handel and Mozart. In them all we find a flight of notes grouped into different spans, each span complementing the others to produce a melodic shape that somehow becomes mysteriously translated into an aesthetic and psychological experience. The melodies of much non-Western music, moving often in spans of vast length, provide almost the only element in such an experience; in Western music they are only one of several elements and appreciated as part of a complex of events.

One of the most satisfying musical shapes is the arch, shown to perfection in the music of Palestrina and other sixteenth-century composers. The gradual ascent to the peak and the gentle descent to the cadence give to their works a superb sense of poised control. A close affinity exists between this kind of melodic writing and much of that found in the *Leçons de ténèbres* (written over a century and a half later). Indeed, generations of composers in France were quite indifferent to many of the musical innovations taking place in Italy after the Renaissance, so that the seventeenth-century French classical tradition absorbed and retained traits from the earlier period until well on in that century, modifying them as tastes slowly changed. One of these traits was a suave and graceful style of melody which, as we saw, had its origins in the Renaissance lute air. Its character has beeen summed up by French writers of that period by the word '*douceur*' or 'sweet gentleness'. Even Lully's creation of French operatic declamation can be seen merely as an extension of this. While Couperin's overall style is, of course, very different from that of Palestrina, there is an approach to melodic writing in the *Leçons de ténèbres*, particularly in the two solo settings, which in some ways lies closer to renaissance than baroque practice.

We encounter this right at the beginning of the first *Leçon* after the liturgical words (which were not by the Prophet) 'Incipit . . .' and the *vocalise* at *Aleph*. *Quomodo sedet sola civitas* begins very simply and gently – with a total span of forty measures there is no place for impatience. Here we have a superbly shaped line, in performance suffused with the radiance of expressive ornamentation. If not 'tuneful' in the popular sense, it has the subtle allure of an art which reveals its secrets slowly.

Such a melody clearly exhibits a fine sense of musical 'draughtsmanship'. Yet is this sufficient for the setting of such a powerful text? The music of *Quomodo sedet sola civitas* certainly has few tragic overtones, but we must see it in its context, for it is only the beginning – almost like a narration which surveys the scene before entering it. The next movement, *Plorans ploravit*, plunges into an expression of deep anguish. Who could fail to be moved by its long, opening cry as it falls down and down in profound despair:

Ex.6   1st Leçon de ténèbres

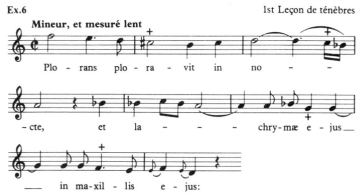

In this movement, as in many others of this work, its expression is frequently intensified by moments of arresting dissonance. At the word *charis* there is a biting false relationship between the D natural of the vocal part and the D sharp of the continuo.

Ex.7   1st Leçon de ténèbres

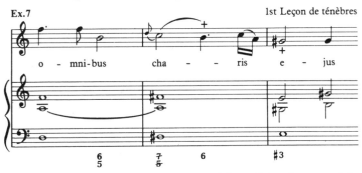

This 'colourful' use of harmony is one of the striking features of the work as a whole, and though it can be interpreted as being an Italian influence on his style (the highly-charged chromaticism of Scarlatti's cantatas would have been well known to Couperin at this time), yet the harmonic aspect of the *Leçons* has a different 'tang', suggesting a style of thinking still essentially French. The kind of harmony evident in Handel's 'Ev'ry Valley' seems almost to have a life of its own, a driving force which propels the melodic phrases to their cadence points, even in slow arias; and what is more, the chromaticism which burgeons from the diatonic processes urges this forward drive even more powerfully. In the French school, even though the harmonic 'syntax' is similar, a good deal of this momentum is missing; one has the feeling that any onward movement is derived from the flow of melody rather than from the flow of harmony. There are instances (as for example in Couperin's organ masses) where the harmony seems almost motionless, the melodic strands alone carrying the music onwards (illustrated in Ex. 3). Now these contrasting practices between French and Italian are very much more a matter of degree than real differences, and in Couperin's music as a whole there is an ever-changing emphasis. In the first two *Leçons*, however, this emphasis is very much upon the French traits described above, while in the third *Leçon* we find greater stylistic variety.

Little more now needs to be said about Couperin's *Leçons de ténèbres* except to point out a few highlights of the work. One of these is the setting of the words *Recordata est Jerusalem* from the second *Leçon*. For it Couperin chose the form of the ground bass, a cyclic method of construction in which the bass repeats the same phrase a number of times while melody and harmony pursue new ideas. In the hands of the masters this tension between the static and the dynamic, the circumscribed and the free, has inspired some of the most eloquent passages in music – one immediately recalls the 'Lament' from Purcell's *Dido and Aeneas*, or the *Crucifixus* from Bach's B Minor Mass – and *Recordata est Jerusalem* is no exception. Its vocal line, seemingly spontaneous and free, searches out the boundaries imposed by the form, and in doing so finds an intensity of expression not usually associated with eighteenth-century French music. Amongst the loveliest passages of the third *Leçon* are the duet setting of the Hebrew letters. Whereas in the first two *Leçons* these short movements acted as little preludes, in the third they are more in the nature of postludes, the main movements flowing into them most usually without a break. At the words *Jerusalem, convertere ad Dominum Deus tuum* at the end of the work Couperin's lyrical inspiration takes wing. The *Leçons de ténèbres* are among the composer's most prized works, bringing the liturgical tradition inherited from the seventeenth century to one of its highest points in French music.

Until recently it was thought that Couperin's output of motets consisted of twenty-two works variously described as *versets*, *motets* and *élévations*. In 1971, however, twelve previously unknown works were discovered in manuscript in the library of St Michael's College, Tenbury, nine of which survive in full. There is no doubt at all about their authenticity, and they have now been published in a modern edition.[1] Together with the incomplete motets from the Tenbury collection and those from all other sources, Couperin's total number of known works in this genre reaches thirty-four.

Those which were published in Couperin's day appeared from 1703 to 1705, after his appointment to the Royal Chapel at Versailles. It is therefore reasonable to regard his entire output of religious vocal music as being the work of his early maturity, for as he grew older so he became increasingly drawn to the music of the salon and chamber, even though he retained his two organ posts almost all his life. Whereas his sombre *Leçons de ténèbres* were written for a closed order of nuns (although they can also be sung in the male register), all his motets were destined for the colourful ceremonies at Versailles, many of them written specifically to exhibit the vocal gifts of the professional singers working at court. The motets, then, are in a style very different from the *Leçons de ténèbres*. Except for one of the movements of the *versets* of 1704, where Couperin requires all the tenors and basses of the Royal Chapel to participate, all his motets were composed for soloists or solo ensembles, many of which had orchestral accompaniment. There are no 'choral' motets.

Those that Couperin called *versets* are settings of chosen verses of a psalm, each verse scored differently from its companions. Some movements are thus virtually independent works. For them the composer enjoyed the services of some of the finest singers of the Chapelle du Roy (such as the two Italian castrati, Hiacinte Mazza and Antonio Paccini, the two basses Abbé Michon and Bastaron) as well as those from the *musique de chambre*, who included Guillaume de Pont (countertenor), Jacques Destival and Du Fau (tenors), Jacques Hyvet de Beaupré (bass), and the two sopranos, Marie Chappe and, above all, his cousin Marguerite-Louise Couperin, who entered the king's service in 1702. For her début as a court

[1] The Tenbury motets have been edited by Philippe Oboussier (who discovered them) in the *Le Pupitre* series (Heugel-Paris).

singer François wrote the motet *Qui dat nivem sicut canon* in which the pretty roulades for voice and flute at the conclusion suggest a voice of lightness and dexterity, qualities confirmed by Titon du Tillet. So too does the opening section of the *Quatre versets*, published the following year, in which the voices of Mlles Couperin and Chappe entwined in a duet emphatically described by the composer as being 'for voices alone, without basso continuo or any other instruments'. When the instruments enter in the later sections the scoring is of the most delicate kind in which the continuo 'bass' is lifted high into the treble register and played by a violin. Indeed, the three collections of *versets* (1703, 1704, 1705) contain most felicitous touchès in their orchestration, as for example in *Dux itinerus fuisti* (a setting of verse 10 from Psalm 74) scored for what the composer described as a *symphonie à deux choeurs*, one group being made up of wind instruments, the other of strings, and providing a delightfully antiphonal style of accompaniment for the bass soloist. The demands that Couperin placed upon his singers was often extreme as in this motet from the Tenbury collection.

Ex.8   (Gayement)   Regina Coeli Laetare

It is clear from these works that the young Couperin was taking full advantage of the vocal resources offered by the court, and revelling in his opportunities, for they reflect as much the quality of his performers as his own musical imagination and technical assurance. Yet it would be a mistake to imagine that Couperin's motets are purely virtuoso pieces. Many of them feature a much simpler style (particularly the *élévations*, performed usually by one or two soloists with organ continuo at one of the most solemn moments in the mass) amongst which are passages of extraordinary beauty, the originality of which is sometimes disguised by their very simplicity. For example, in the *Sept versets* of 1704 the setting of the words from Psalm 84 *Salutare tuum du nobis* (a movement composed for the countertenor Du Four) Couperin conceived a passage of remarkably piquant harmony:

Ex.9   Sept Versets (1704)

Like a number of passages in the *Leçons de ténèbres* this kind of writing seems to embody a very French approach to harmony – the use of dissonance for the purposes of 'colour' rather than 'harmonic function'. Nevertheless the motets written for Versailles were also often Italianate. And no wonder, for what appears to be his first motet, *Laudate pueri Dominum*, was written only two or three years after his youthful encounter with the sonatas of Corelli and his subsequent (and successful) attempt to write a group of trio sonatas in the Italian manner.

Chamber Music

LES NATIONS

Although it was not until the last eleven years of his life that Couperin actually began publishing any instrumental ensemble music, his interest in this genre stemmed from his earliest years as a composer when, like so many of his generation in France, he was fired with enthusiasm for the newly-discovered Italian instrumental style. This we learn from his account of the genesis of *Les Nations*, a collection of four extended trio sonatas published in 1726. Its preface is worth reproducing in full.

It is a few years now since one part of these trios was composed; a few manuscripts of them were distributed about, but I have little faith in them because of the negligence of the copyists. From time to time I have added to their number, and I believe that lovers of the true will find them to their liking. The first Sonata in this collection is also the first that I composed and the first of its kind to be composed in France. It has quite a singular story.

Charmed by the sonatas of Signor Corelli and the French works of M. de Lulli, both of whose compositions I shall love as long as I live, I ventured to compose a sonata myself which I had played by the same group as I had heard play Corelli's. Knowing how keen the French are on foreign novelties in all matters, and lacking confidence in myself, I did myself a favour through an inoffensive stratagem. I pretended that a relative of mine that I actually do have and who is attached to the court of the King of Sardinia, had sent me a sonata by a new Italian composer. I arranged the letters of my name so as to form an Italian name which I gave instead. The sonata was received with much acclaim and I will say nothing further in its defence. I wrote others and my italianised name brought me, wearing this mask, great applause. Fortunately my sonatas enjoyed sufficient favour for me not to blush at my subterfuge. I have compared these first sonatas with others that I have written since and have not changed or added anything much. I have simply added some long suites to which the sonatas act as preludes or introductions.

I hope that the unbiased public will be pleased with them. For there are always prejudiced fault-finders who are more to be feared than those who criticise fairly, for these often unintentionally give some very good advice.

The former are despicable and I am always ready to return anything they give me with interest. I have a sufficiently great number of these trios to make another volume of them later on as complete as this one.

Comments by Couperin found elsewhere suggest that some of these early works which found their way into *Les Nations* (forming, as Couperin says, the opening movements to the four suites which were written at a much later date) were composed as early as 1692. This was eleven years after the appearance of Corelli's influential first set of trio sonatas of 1681, and Couperin's youthful essays are clearly indebted to them.

The trio sonata had been cultivated in Italy in one form or another, and under various descriptions (canzona, canzona da sonare, sonata, sinfonia, etc.) throughout much of the century.[1] Its essential features lay in its texture: two upper instruments accompanied by a basso continuo. The latter might join in the fugal interplay of the upper parts or simply provide a treading bass. The growing popularity of the violin in Italy led to it becoming the preferred instrument in the trio sonata, although works calling for flutes, oboes, recorders and other melody-type instruments were frequent. The basso continuo was provided by harpsichord or organ partnered by cello, the performance thus requiring an ensemble of four players even though the composer provided only three parts.[2] By the time of Corelli the trio sonata had taken two paths which, although eventually to converge again, had developed distinctive traits: those of the *sonata da chiesa* (church sonata) and the *sonata da camera* (chamber sonata). The distinction was as much one of function as of style, for the *sonata da chiesa* was performed during church services at moments such as the offertory. As might be expected, the *sonata da chiesa* tended to be more serious in style than the *sonata da camera*, having much resource to fugal devices and the processes of thematic development. The *sonata da camera* on the other hand employed the forms and styles of the dance. Towards the end of the seventeenth century, however, these distinctions broke down. Yet whether for church or chamber, the trio sonata in its fully developed style was indebted to two major influences: the violin and the voice, the fast movements using themes moulded by techniques natural to the agile stringed instrument, the slow move-

---

[1] See Christopher Hogwood, *The Trio Sonata* (BBC Music Guide Series, 1979).

[2] On occasions the continuo partnership has two distinctly different parts.

45

ments filled with a lyrical expression that sprang from the bel canto aria. Such was the flexibility of the medium that the trio sonata was cultivated in Italy more widely than any other instrumental form.

On the other hand, France (like England) had cultivated the viol fantasia as the central medium of instrumental chamber music during the seventeenth century, although the contrapuntal and 'learned' style inherited from the fantasias of the Renaissance gave way in the middle of the century to the simpler style of the dance suite. French regard for viols remained high throughout the whole century, virtuosi like Sainte-Colombe and Marin Marais helping to maintain the status of the instrument in France long after it had surrendered to the violin and cello elsewhere. In fact, as late as the beginning of the eighteenth century, the violin was still regarded in some quarters as a mere street instrument. While Couperin retained a deep affection for the viol, his trio sonatas provide a fine medium for the violin although the instrument itself is not usually specified on the score. It is typical of Couperin's sonatas that the upper parts are described as being for *'dessus'*, i.e. treble instruments. Yet in some of the fast movements it is hard to escape the feeling that they were truly inspired by Corelli's violin writing, as in the following excerpt which makes great use of that athletic style developed by Italian violinists:

Ex.10   L'Impériale

It is in passages such as these with their driving rhythms and sequentially shaped phrases that Couperin's trio sonatas most obviously reveal their debt to Corelli and the Italian school. We may well ask whether in his enthusiasm Couperin has betrayed his own musical personality? We can answer this best by comparing a movement from Corelli's Op. 1, no. 3 with one from *La Françoise* which employs almost identical thematic material (Ex. 11 opposite). It seems clear that Couperin was basing his work upon the model of Corelli's, and yet, despite obvious similarities, a performance of

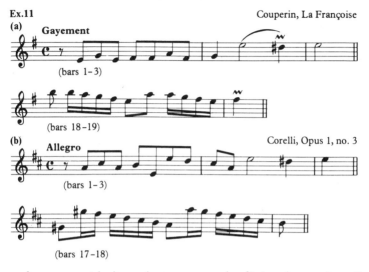

Ex.11 Couperin, La Françoise
(a) Gayement
(bars 1–3)
(bars 18–19)
(b) Allegro Corelli, Opus 1, no. 3
(bars 1–3)
(bars 17–18)

each movement in its entirety conveys the distinct impression of two different musical personalities. In the working out of this material, for example, Corelli the violinist lets his string technique take over much of the thematic development, expanding the phrases to a degree not followed by Couperin. Even in the simple scale passages Corelli covers a wider span than does Couperin (Ex. 12 overleaf). Such points of difference are small – as indeed we would expect when one composer sought to emulate the other. Nevertheless they reflect, albeit dimly, those unconscious attitudes to musical style inherited by each composer. This as much prevented Couperin's most Italianate works from sounding like slavish imitations of Corelli as it saved Purcell's personality when, 'in just imitation of the most fam'd Italian masters', he had composed his trio sonatas of 1683 and 1697. In Couperin's works the less expansive phrase and the preference for stepwise movement are characteristic of the French approach which almost always sought suaveness and grace, qualities still present in Couperin's trio sonatas despite their vivacity and energy.

If we turn to the slow movements the differences are much greater. Apart from the ornamentation (which, if we are to judge from the one surviving manuscript copy of the original versions of *c*. 1692, was largely missing when Couperin had the work per-

Ex.12

(a)

Couperin, La Françoise

(b)

Corelli, Opus 1, no. 3

(bars 11–15)

formed as an 'Italian' piece) we are aware of a different kind of lyricism from that which came spontaneously from Corelli. Nevertheless it is, of course, possible to find whole passages in the sonatas of Couperin and Corelli where the convergence of their styles outweighs differences. In general terms, however, while there are similarities of style, the overall impression of distinctive musical personalities remains.

Les Nations comprises what Couperin called four *ordres* (meaning a self-contained collection of pieces), each one falling into two parts: a *sonata da chiesa* (the earlier composed trio sonatas) and a *sonata da camera* (i.e. a suite of dance movements). The full title reads

LES NATIONS
SONADES et Suites de SIMPHONIES
EN TRIO
En quatre Livres Séparés pour la Comodité
des Académies de Musique
Et des Concerts particuliers

and they appear in the following order:

Premier Ordre	Second Ordre
La Françoise	*L'Espagnole*
(originally called	(originally called
La Pucelle)	*La Visionnaire*)
Allemande	Allemande
Première Courante	Courante
Seconde Courante	Seconde Courante
Sarabande	Sarabande
Gigue	Gigue Lourée
Chaconne ou Passacaille	Gavotte
Gavotte	Rondeau
Menuet	Bourée
	Passacaille
Troisième Ordre	Quatrième Ordre
L'Impériale	*La Piédmontoise*
	(originally called *L'Astrée*)
Allemande	Allemande
Courante	Courante
Seconde Courante	Seconde Courante
Sarabande	Sarabande
Bourrée	Rondeau
Gigue	Gigue
Rondeau	
Chaconne	
Menuet	

It will be seen that each of the four *ordres* is a sizeable work, and all the more so in that the trio sonatas alone each comprise six to nine movements. (*L'Impériale* is twice as long as any trio sonata by Corelli.) If, in the tradition of the *sonata da chiesa*, Couperin avoids the dance forms in his opening sonatas, the spirit of the dance is never far away, especially in the slow movements. It was, of course, in the movements which follow the trio sonatas that Couperin's French manner (now given full rein as there was no need to hide his identity) stood in strong relief to Corelli's style – and this even when the Italian master employed the dance forms derived from France. If Corelli's penchant for the 'sonata style' helped mould his dance movements, the converse was true for Couperin.

The preface to *Les Nations* tells of the composer's plan to compile another collection of similar works, as he already had 'a sufficiently great number of trios' to form the basis. No such volume appeared, but amongst those which he may have had in mind to incorporate in the second collection could have been *La Superbe* and *La Stein-querque*, two trio sonatas left unpublished at his death. The latter piece, however, is one of his few disappointing works, being a 'battle-piece' written to celebrate the victory of the Maréchal de Luxembourg over William III in 1692. There is yet another work, and a very fine one, which remained unpublished: *La Sultane*; but it is very doubtful if Couperin was referring to this as it is a quartet and not a trio sonata. Couperin was to publish a considerable amount of chamber music, but the only other trio sonatas beyond those already mentioned were his homages to Lully and Corelli. It is these masterworks to which we next turn.

LE PARNASSE OU L'APOTHÉOSE DE CORELLI

Some thirty years separate Couperin's trio sonatas emulating the example of Corelli and those which he wrote in tribute to the same composer in 1724. *Le Parnasse ou L'Apothéose de Corelli* appeared at a time when Couperin's publications were exclusively in the field of instrumental ensemble music (1722 to 1728). The composer was now in his middle fifties, his reputation at its height and his genius in full bloom. By this time his publications included the *Leçons de ténèbres*, three of the four books of harpsichord pieces and the treatise *L'Art de toucher le clavecin*. After this period only the final book of harpsichord pieces was to come. *L'Apothéose de Corelli* is thus one of the works of his maturity, and as such it forms an interesting comparison with the early trio sonatas.

Far from inhibiting the Italianate gestures, Couperin's advancing years seem to have strengthened them. Certainly *L'Apothéose de Corelli* reveals a fuller grasp of the foreign style than do his early trio sonatas. Its opening movement, for example, mirrors the expansiveness and the melodic figuration of an Italian *grave*, the wide and expressive leaps standing in contrast to the simple lines of the opening of *La Françoise (La Pucelle)*.

Ex.13   L'Apothéose de Corelli

Later movements catch the brilliance of the Italian instrumental style to a degree not encountered in the earlier pieces. On the other hand the wit and picturesque nature of the work, as well as its ornamentation, are characteristically French. Perhaps, above all, its provenance is revealed through its programmatic nature. Thus the first movement is entitled 'Corelli, at the foot of Parnassus, begs the Muses to receive him into their company', and the vivacious fugal movement which follows expresses his pleasure on being welcomed and admitted. The picture 'Corelli drinking at the Fountain of Hippocrene' (traditionally the well-springs of art) is painted in one of Couperin's loveliest movements. In it a little undulating figure suggestive of the rippling waters is set against a slower-moving phrase, and from these simplest of materials emerges music of extraordinary beauty. Cast in a simple form in which the ideas constantly return, its texture is one of seemingly endless variety as the phrases flow from one voice to another in every conceivable combination: now in imitation, now together; first in one register, then another. Seemingly so simple and artless, it is the finely distilled product of imagination and craftsmanship of the first order (Ex. 14).

Having drunk of the waters of Hippocrene, Corelli's enthusiasm finds outlet in an energetic and brilliant trio sonata. Tired from his exertions, Corelli sleeps while his companions play a gentle piece – this very much in the French style. Wakened by the Muses, Corelli is placed next to Apollo during the accompaniment of a brilliant fanfare-like movement, after which he gives thanks in an energetic piece featuring a fine syncopated fugal subject. With *L'Apothéose de Corelli*, Couperin's debt to the Italian master is fully paid.

L'APOTHÉOSE COMPOSÉ À LA MÉMOIRE DE L'INCOMPARABLE MONSIEUR DE LULLY

In the following year (1725) Couperin published his homage to Lully in which he also paid further tribute to Corelli by placing both musicians together on the heights of Parnassus. Seemingly the very embodiment of Italian and French music of the time, the two composers were, however, not exact contemporaries, Lully belonging to a slightly earlier generation: Corelli outlived him by nearly thirty years. In fact *L'Apothéose de Corelli* was published only nine years after Corelli's death. Yet despite the difference of age, both men were

Ex.14

L'Apothéose de Corelli

essentially composers of the mid-Baroque who consolidated the techniques of late-seventeenth-century music in their countries, and provided the basis for the next and final stage of that style era. As far as French music was concerned *L'Apothéose de Lully*, together with much of Couperin's other music, is representative of this last phase. If its new concepts are implicit in the music, some of the fanciful titles to the movements of this work define the new style quite clearly, and in so doing make explicit his ideals of unifying French and Italian styles.

Like *L'Apothéose de Corelli* the work has a programmatic element, the title of each movement being as follows:

Lully in the Elysian Fields performing with musicianly Shades

Air for the same performers

Mercury's flight to the Elysian Fields to warn that Apollo is about to descend

The descent of Apollo who comes to offer his violin to Lully and a place on Parnassus

Subterranean rumblings from Lully's contemporaries

Laments from the same, played by flutes or very sweet-toned instruments

The raising of Lully to Parnassus

Welcome – half friendly, half hostile – given to Lully by Corelli and the Italian Muses

Lully's thanks to Apollo

Apollo persuades Lully and Corelli that the bringing together of French and Italian styles must create musical perfection

Air léger (Lully playing the melody, Corelli accompanying him)

Second Air (Corelli playing the melody, Lully accompanying him)

The Peace of Parnassus which, following a protest from the French Muses, is made on condition that when their language is spoken there one will henceforth say *Sonade* and *Cantade*, as one says *Ballade* and *Sérénade*

As well as giving us some of Couperin's most attractive pages, *L'Apothéose de Lully* provides a witty commentary in music on the two main national styles of the day. The significance of Couperin's subtly allusive writing in this work should be clear. As might be expected from their titles, the first seven movements are wholly French in style. Thus, the scene of the Elysian Fields (Ex. 15) is painted through music redolent of that 'sweet languor' of the *goût français*, its simple, smooth melody wreathed in profuse but delicate ornamentation.

The graceful air which follows it is moulded by the gestures of the dance, while the appearance of Mercury is heralded by the kind of picturesque figuration which Lully himself had so often used to suggest the rush of wind or the play of zephyrs, as can be seen in Ex. 16 overleaf.

Ex.15

Similarly, while greater demands are certainly placed upon some of the instruments than are found in the scores of Lully, the 'subterranean rumblings' could have come from many a page of his *tragédies lyriques*. And yet, through its delicate scoring and exquisite ornamentation, the Lament conveys so much by the most economical of means:

Ex.17

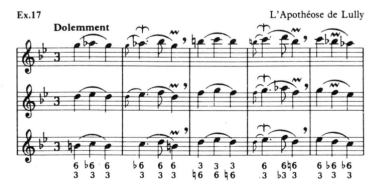

With the appearance of Corelli and the Italian Muses who welcome Lully to Parnassus a subtle change steals over the music, for the solemn opening of a *sonata da chiesa* (significantly, marked *largo* in place of *gravement*) is sounded, and there ensues a movement rich in motivic figuration, entwined suspensions and counterpoint, all supported by the treading bass of the continuo. Like many an Italian movement, this one immediately repeats its opening statement in a new key (cf. Ex. 21, p. 65), and to ensure an Italianate performance the players are instructed to avoid the French habit of altering the rhythm through *notes inégales* (see p. 20), the score being marked *notes égales et marquées*.

Lully's reply to this Italian welcome stands in firm contrast and we are back to the world of courtly charm, although Couperin goes considerably further than did Lully in the art of ornamentation and the extension of musical ideas.

Apollo's conviction that the union of French and Italian styles will bring about the 'perfection of music' is demonstrated in what Couperin describes as an *Essai en forme d'Ouverture* played by the two composers and their respective Muses, accompanied of course by a continuo. The French Overture, invented by Lully and adopted by composers outside France, commenced in a majestic style proclaimed by strong, 'dotted' rhythms, this giving way to a faster section which in the hands of Italian and German composers became the vehicle for vigorous fugal writing and instrumental display. So, in the *Essai* we find Lully's style in evidence in the opening section, and Corelli's in the second; as a compliment to each other both composers and their Muses play very largely in unison, as though to show that each is capable of playing like the

Ex.16

(a)

Cadmus et Hermione (Lully)

L'Envie distribue des serpents aux Vents qui forment autour d'elle des manières de tourbillons.

Entrée de L'Envie

(b)

L'Apothéose de Lully

other. Thus, the first section having paid tribute to the originator of the form, the second offers homage to Corelli and the Italian sonata style.

After this it is time not merely to juxtapose the two styles but to fuse them together, and the two Airs which follow the Overture accomplish this in a delightfully witty way. The music is a duet (without basso continuo) between Lully and Corelli. The Frenchman leads off with a terse fugue-like subject and, as though bowing in response to this most tactful opening gambit, Corelli replies with the same. The courtesies having been observed, Lully's theme dissolves into a sweet and flowing melody adorned with *coulades* (those typically French embellishments which add smoothness to expressiveness) while Corelli develops the sonata-style opening into an accompaniment largely made up of arpeggios and wholly devoid of ornamentation. It is only in the second half of this Air that Lully adjusts his style to catch the Italian spirit of his partner.

The roles of melodist and accompanist are then exchanged for the second Air. The key now being minor, Corelli can exploit something of that famous Italian pathos, this reaching its peak four measures from the end in the chromatic chord of the so-called 'Neapolitan sixth', while the melody itself gains a new degree of expansiveness. Unlike Corelli's accompaniment in the previous Air, Lully's is filled with those smooth, flowing lines characteristic of the French style, until in the second half he once more adjusts his style to that of his partner.

Ex.18   L'Apothéose de Lully

On joue ces 2 Airs deux
fois chacun alternativement.

Convinced by this demonstration, all the musicians are called upon to execute a splendid finale (described, of course, by the newly-coined term *Sonade en trio*) in which French and Italian styles join together to confirm Apollo's declaration that with their union may be achieved the perfection of music.

It might be asked if *L'Apothéose de Lully* is a mere pastiche in which Couperin's musical personality is largely withdrawn in order to serve the poetic programme. The answer is an emphatic no. In this work, as well as in *L'Apothéose de Corelli* and *Les Nations*, Couperin absorbed the Italian manner into his own technique which remained always the servant of his peculiarly French imagination. Even when recalling the Lullian tradition it was the spirit rather than the letter of his style which Couperin sought, for indeed he put words into Lully's mouth, so to speak, that the older master would have rejected. Take the question of ornamentation, for example. As we saw in pp. 14–15, Lully was not drawn to the rich style of embellishment much in vogue in *Les vingt-quatre violons du Roy* at the time of his arrival from Florence, and when given his own orchestra (*Les petits violons*) he trained it to play in a clean and incisive way that became famous throughout Europe.* Even in his vocal music there is little ornamentation, for his was the heroic gesture of the *tragédie lyrique*. The style of ornamentation which we most usually associate with the French school sprang from the more intimate music of the salon – lute airs and harpsichord suites.

Couperin was the chamber musician *par excellence*, and his works inevitably exploited the subtle art of ornamentation, even in those pages of the present work where he invoked the grand presence of Lully. *L'Apothéose de Lully* is, then, not a work in imitation but in true homage.

CONCERTS ROYAUX AND NOUVEAUX CONCERTS

In 1722 Couperin published the first of two volumes of instrumental ensemble music in a genre different from the trio sonata. The initial volume was entitled *Concerts royaux*, by which name the works had been known at court where they had been performed nearly ten years earlier. The aged King enjoyed them so much that he commanded Couperin and his fellow musicians to play from the collection nearly every Sunday during the years 1714 and 1715. The *Concerts royaux* were, in fact, to be Couperin's last works written specially for Versailles, for after Louis XIV's death in 1715 the composer moved back to Paris permanently.

Two years after the publication of the *Concerts royaux* another collection of similar pieces appeared, sharing the same volume as *L'Apothéose de Corelli* and entitled *Les Goûts réunis ou Nouveaux concerts*. Perhaps had the first collection not been dubbed '*Concerts royaux*' by members of the court Couperin might have described all of them as suites or *ordres*, for that is precisely what they are. Each *Concert* commences with a Prelude and is followed by dances or other movements and in a particular key. He composed four *Concerts royaux* and ten *Nouveaux concerts*; we shall refer to the fourteen sets simply as *Concerts*, giving to each the number in order of appearance irrespective of which collection they come from, for they comprise a single genre.

For the royal performances of the earlier collection, Couperin at the harpsichord had been joined by the violinist François Duval, André Danican Philidor who played oboe and bassoon (amongst a number of instruments), Hilaire Verloge (also known as Alarius) who was a bass violist, and the bassoonist Dubois. Yet in fact the majority of the fourteen *Concerts* were composed without specific instrumentation in mind, most of them being set out on two staves only – like a keyboard piece. More usually the upper stave contains only one line of melody, but it may also contain two. Almost any of the usual '*dessus*' instruments (flute, oboe, violin, treble viol, etc.)

may play these, although some movements seem to suggest by the style of writing that Couperin may have had in mind a particular instrument not specified on the score. The lower stave usually comprises a single bass part which, with its figured harmony, is obviously most appropriate for harpsichord either alone or with bass viol (or cello) or bassoon. Couperin also alludes to the possibility of using *théorbe* (bass lute) in place of harpsichord. Indeed so flexible is the scoring that almost all the pieces can – as Couperin suggests – be played by harpsichord alone.

Nevertheless, on occasion – sometimes for single movements, sometimes for complete works – Couperin does indicate some preference in instrumentation, the viols being favourites. In the twelfth *Concert*, written for 'two viols or other equal instruments' (*instruments à l'unisson*), the composer goes further than in most of the other works by suggesting that this particular *Concert* sounds at its best without any harpsichord or *théorbe*, underlining the recommendation by not providing a figured bass (except in the Prelude where some accompanied passages are set off in contrast to those marked *'viols sans accompagnement'*. The *Concerts* are thus remarkable for the freedom of choice in the way of instrumentation, and on this score alone should be more familiar than they are to performers of baroque ensemble music. But more than this, they should be more widely known because of the fascination of the music itself.

As suggested by the title of the 1724 collection – *Les Goûts réunis* – the *Concerts* bring together a rich variety of styles. While only one movement makes overt reference to Italy (Courante italienne, fourth *Concert*) many of the characteristics of her music are woven into the overall style of the works; these *Concerts* remain, however, unquestionably the product of a French musical mind. The collection commences with one of Couperin's finest lyrical inspirations – a solemn melody of Bach-like nobility and spaciousness. Yet its long-breathed phrases are shaped not through the typical Italian/German processes of motivic development, but through the infinite variation of three basic shapes or gestures which are present throughout the entire movement. As the expressive and rich ornamentation tends to hide these seminal sources, the three shapes (marked a, b, c) are set out separately from the melody in the next example. Space forbids all but the opening measures of this wonderful Prelude (Ex. 19 overleaf).

Not every *Concert* commences with an air of such nobility; some opening movements (*Concert* nos. 2, 5, 9, 13) strike a far lighter note. But in all cases, the Preludes afford Couperin the opportunity to draw out his lyrical gifts in forms far freer than those of the dance movements with their sectional structures and stylised rhythms.

The first of the more stylised movements following a Prelude is usually an Allemande. We know that this dance originated in Germany, probably in the fifteenth century, and that by 1588 was rather sedate (*'médiocre gravité'* is the description given by Arbeau in *Orchésographie*, his famous dance treatise of that year). Yet a dance-notated Allemande which has come down to us from the end of the seventeenth century suggests that by then it was light and graceful.[1] So varied is the music that bears the title during its long history that it is very difficult to characterise its style. Moreover, to add to the confusion, it would seem that the Allemande as ballroom dance and Allemande as instrumental piece parted company some time during the seventeenth century. What characteristics the instrumental form may have acquired in France at this time very often disappeared entirely when it was transplanted to suites composed elsewhere, as in the trio sonatas of Corelli where one Allemande is marked to be played *grave* and the next *presto*. One is forced to the conclusion that in such cases the composer merely applied the term to a movement in duple or quadruple time which appeared fairly early in the order of dances in a suite or sonata.

In the keyboard music of the mid-seventeenth-century harpsichord composer Chambonnières the Allemande is usually characterised by a quadruple metre and a melody flowing in semiquavers, often beginning with an up-beat. The tempo of such pieces is largely determined by the fairly luxuriant ornamentation indi-

[1] Pierre Rameau, *Danses de ville* (Paris, 1725), pp. 58–64.

cated by this composer, but the spirit seems close to Arbeau's *médiocre gravité*. As we shall see in the next chapter, all of Couperin's keyboard Allemandes are in the Chambonnières tradition and contain some of his most profound and striking pages. In his *Concerts*, however, only one (no. 10) catches this noble spirit. Most of the others, marked *légèrement* or *vivement*, are far more fleet-footed. But what is even more striking (in comparison with his keyboard movements) is that, in keeping with the title *Les Goûts réunis*, more than half the Allemandes in the *Concerts* take up a truly Corellian stance and, commencing with fugal entries, are far more like sonata than dance movements. Indeed the second *Concert* contains a movement actually called *Allemande fuguée*, a title which Couperin could have applied quite widely to a number of pieces. Couperin's term *fuguée* should not be taken too seriously, for his contrapuntal designs are very free and, unlike Bach's fugues, are apt to lapse into a lively melodic figure with bass accompaniment occasionally unified by snatches of imitation here and there. Even the impressively titled *Air contrafugué* from the same concert as the *Allemande fuguée* is in no way as alarming as its name might suggest. In this delightful piece Couperin merely plays one half of the theme against the other half and, although the movement demonstrates some textbook counterpoint, Couperin's learning is worn so lightly that the music gives the impression only of good-humoured badinage.

It is only in the *Fugueté* of the final *Concert* that a purer contrapuntal style is sustained, and in the imitative working out of material Couperin gives us passages of striking chromaticism:

Ex.20   ´14th Concert

As this work gathers momentum there appears a figure which, while suitable for violin, also inevitably reminds one of the passage-work in many a Bach organ fugue. So do the opening and closing movements of this collection of fourteen *Concerts* catch something of the northern spirit as well as the southern, attesting the success of Couperin's aim of bringing together the musical styles of his day.

If, in the main, the national styles become so fused as to become one, the *Concerts* also contain two dance forms which Couperin sets apart: the French and Italian versions of the Courante, their juxtaposition found in the fourth *Concert*. The Italian Corranto, originating in the sixteenth century, was a lively dance in triple metre commencing with an up-beat. Couperin provides us with a classic example, its Italianism strengthened through the imitative entries at the beginning of each section.

Ex.21   4th Concert

The French Courante, on the other hand, was far more sophisticated in its rhythm, fluctuating between a duple and a triple grouping of notes, a device known as hemiola. While the first measures can be heard in groupings of either twos or threes, the fifth is clearly a triple metre (Ex. 22 overleaf).

Another dance which featured the hemiola rhythm was the Loure (a much slower dance than the Courante), an example of which is the eighth *Concert*. Sub-titled *dans le goût théâtral*, this *Concert* is one of the longest in the collection and, appropriately, commences not with a Prelude but with a French Overture suggestive of the grandeur of the stage rather than the intimacy of the salon. In the

fugal section of this Overture, Couperin very cleverly gives the impression that there are more than two voices taking part by sounding the bass voice first at a high level and then dropping into a lower register for each succeeding fugal entry. Another form reserved for this *Concert* is a *Grande Ritornèle*, the term borrowed from the *tragédie lyrique* where it fulfilled the role of an orchestral interlude. Apart from these two movements it is perhaps the preponderance of airs (six in all) and the absence of the Allemande and Courante (rarely found in the *tragédie lyrique*) that imparts a 'theatrical' flavour to this work, together with the final 'scene' depicting the followers of Bacchus in a gay frolic.

More programmatic than the *Concert dans le goût théâtral* – at least as far as picturesque titles is concerned – is the Italian-named ninth *Concert*: *Ritratto dell' Amore* (Portrait of Love). Most of its movements (with titles in French!) are dances, even if they are not specified as such. Thus we have *L'Enjouement* (a 'Corellian'-type Allemande), *Les Grâces* (French Courante), *La Noble fierté* (Sarabande), *La Douceur* (Forlane), *L'et Coetera* (Minuets). Only *Le je-ne-scay-quoi* and *La Vivacité* are not obviously dances, while the unsectionalised structure of the opening movement, *Le Charme*, provides a parallel with the Preludes of other *Concerts*.

Among the dance forms employed in the fourteen *Concerts* are: Rigaudon, Sarabande, Gavotte, Menuet, Forlane, Sicilienne, Loure, Chaconne (all of which are described in the Appendix), and they carry some of Couperin's most imaginative and picturesque ideas. The Sarabandes in nos. 3, 9 and 12 are very powerful works, while the Forlane of no. 4 is among the composer's most enchanting creations.

The rondeau, with its recurring refrain and so-called *couplets* (or intervening 'episodes') was a favourite form of Couperin and under this heading come *Echos* (no. 2), *Chaconne légère* (no. 3), *Musète dans le goût de Carillon* (no. 5), *Air tendre* (no. 8), and *Rondeau* (no. 10).

The *Musète dans le goût de Carillon* stands in strong contrast to the *Muzette* of the third *Concert*. With its bass drone sounding throughout, the latter is typical of the so-called *musette* in which a certain rustic simplicity is achieved through imitation of the little bagpipe of the same name. The *Musète dans le goût de Carillon*, while free from the restriction of an actual drone, still conveys something of its effect by the reiteration of short phrases and repetitive harmony suggestive of peals of bells.

Ex.23   3rd Concert

This gift for translating a picturesque idea into apt musical terms is something we shall encounter time and time again in Couperin's keyboard works and while the pieces can be always enjoyed on a purely musical level there can be little doubt that Couperin's audience delighted in associating the two. Take, for example, the *Plainte* from the tenth *Concert*. While an Italian composer would most likely convey the expression of deep sadness through the resources of rich (probably chromatic) harmonies and poignant melody, Couperin conjures up the almost *physical presence* of weeping, and this by the simplest means: a little figure that tries convulsively to rise, falling back each time to the same level as though powerless to shake off some overwhelming grief.

Ex.24

Lentement, et douloureusement   10th Concert

Couperin preferred that viols should play this piece. Indeed, as the works were composed, one by one they moved more and more into the province of the viol. It was to be the instrument with which Couperin closed his output of chamber music.

PIÈCES DE VIOLES

Couperin was sixty-one when he published his *Pièces de violes* in 1728. It was to be his penultimate publication, and although at the time of his death he possessed eleven copies of it, only one is known to have survived. Unlike the title-pages to his other published works, which boldly spell out his name and the positions he held, that to the *Pièces de violes* was unusually reticent, giving as the composer's name only Mr F.C., and it was not until 1922 that these works were recognised as being by François Couperin,[1] even though his full name was spelled out in the royal *privilège* which granted him permission to publish them.

The publications comprise two suites for solo bass viol accompanied by continuo (harpsichord together with another bass viol). In place of terms such as *ordre*, *sonade*, *concert*, Couperin returns to the word *suite*, the first of these containing Prelude, Allemande légère, Courante (Italian style), Sarabande grave, Gavotte, Gigue and Passacaille or Chaconne, while the second contains Prelude, Fuguette, *Pompe funèbre* and *La Chemise blanche*. We have already

---

[1] They were identified in 1922 by Charles Bouvet. As well as being published in the L'Oiseau-Lyre Edition of the Complete Works, the *Pièces de violes* have recently been edited by Lucy Robinson for the *Le Pupitre* series (Heugel-Paris). See also Julia Anne Sadie, *The Bass Viol in French Chamber Music* (Michigan, 1980).

seen Couperin's use of viols in some of his *Concerts*, but the writing found in the two suites springs from a quite different tradition: that of the virtuoso solo violist whose standards had been set in the seventeenth century by men like Sainte-Colombe, Foqueray, Marin Marais, Jean Rousseau and others.[1] Such playing demanded not only extreme agility but also the mastery of a wide variety of ornamentation (including special kinds of vibrato) and the ability to play chords on the instrument. To increase the range of the bass viol French makers added a seventh (bass) string, giving the instrument an effective range of three and a half octaves from low A to e''. (Couperin takes the part up to d'' in *La Chemise blanche*.) The demands made upon the player by these and other works in the solo virtuoso repertoire has, of course, meant that Couperin's magnificent *Pièces de violes* are not widely known, but with the recent emergence of many fine players these works have a much better chance than ever before.

VOCAL CHAMBER MUSIC

Under this heading come the twelve secular songs for one or more voices which Couperin wrote at various times in the middle years of his career, nine of them being published in Ballard's famous monthly collection, *Recueils d'airs sérieux et à boire*. A seemingly insatiable appetite for amorous and convivial songs had developed in France during the seventeenth century and the presses of the Ballard family worked hard to satisfy it, turning out each year hundreds of *airs à boire*, *airs sérieux*, *airs tendres*, *brunettes*, and so on. While the drinking songs (*airs à boire*) were easily identifiable by their texts (enjoying a greater freedom from the restrictions of poetic 'taste' than did the others) a blurred line only separated the various categories of amorous songs. What was common to all, including the convivial ones, was their musical simplicity. In this regard, Couperin's contribution to the genre was no exception. Only in the florid variations which sometimes followed the first verse (known as *doubles* or *diminutions*) did the air challenge any but the most elementary vocal technique.

[1] See Celia Pond, 'Ornamental style and the virtuoso: solo bass viol music in France *c.* 1680–1740', *Early Music* (OUP), vol. 6, no. 4, October 1978, and John Hsu, 'The use of the bow in French solo viol playing of the 17th and 18th centuries' in the same issue of *Early Music*.

His first air, *Qu'on ne me dise*, appeared in the March issue of Ballard's recueils for 1697 and was written for solo voice with continuo. Three other such songs appeared in 1701, 1711 and 1712, including one (*Doux lieux de mon coeur*) that used as a text the translation of a duet by Scarlatti which had been published in the same collection the previous month. Four vocal duets (one without continuo) include the setting of some delightful lines by La Fontaine called *Epitaphe d'un paresseux* (Epitaph to a lazy man). Finally, there are four trios, one of which (*Faison du temps*) was published in 1712 as a *vaudeville*, a term which meant at that time a song in popular style. Couperin's trio has all the heartiness of a drinking song without its characteristic text.

There remain three unpublished trios: *Trois Vestales champêtres et trois Policons*, *La Femme entre deux draps* and *A moy! tout est perdu*. Apart from their musical worth, the first two help to round out Couperin's personality for us, giving it perhaps a more human quality than is suggested by his aristocratic art; for if the first of these trios has indecent overtones, the second – a three-part canon – is explicitly bawdy! Of the three, the musical palm must go to *A moy! tout est perdu*, a splendidly conceived canon or round, the most remarkable feature of which is the textural variety which has been 'built in' to the piece through the imaginative construction of the long opening phrase of the leading voice.

Two of the solo songs – *La Pastorale* and *Les Pellerines* – we shall meet again in the first book of harpsichord pieces published a year later.

Music for Harpsichord

To claim that Couperin is best known as a harpsichord composer is not at all to say that – beyond a handful of pieces – his music for the instrument is widely known. This is not surprising, for it is only in very recent years that his complete works for harpsichord have been recorded on long-playing records, and the chances of hearing concert performances of a good cross-section of them, while improving, are still relatively rare. Moreover, while almost all the harpsichord music of Bach and a fair proportion of Scarlatti's transfers quite readily to the piano, Couperin's loses much of its essential character this way; and thus his music has not passed to any extent into the hands of pianists, domestic or professional. In any case, it is highly doubtful whether, had this happened, it would have well served the composer.

Even if the appropriate instrument is available (and in these days of relatively inexpensive kits based upon the best eighteenth-century models this is no longer an insurmountable problem) Couperin does not make it easy for the performer. Despite the long list of ornaments and their execution which he placed at the beginning of the first book of harpsichord pieces, he has a fondness for using at least one sign which does not appear in it, and even his invaluable *L'Art de toucher le clavecin* leaves unanswered a number of fundamental questions relative as much to French baroque practice in general as to Couperin's keyboard music. The technical demands posed by the ornamentation alone are daunting, to say the least; and these, together with the challenges of many of the brilliant or virtuoso pieces, partly account for the reason why Couperin's harpsichord music is not as well known as that of his German and Italian contemporaries. Lastly, a fine harpsichord technique is in itself no guarantee of a fine performance of Couperin's music; this ultimately rests upon a knowledge of and a feeling for the French style. Exactly the same could, of course, be said about performing the music of the French harpsichord school as a whole.

Indeed it would be mistaken to view Couperin in isolation from the tradition which nourished his art, and equally wrong to regard his predecessors – Chambonnières, D'Anglebert, Louis Couperin (his uncle) and many others – as merely paving the way for him. They did this, of course; but while the younger man was to make the art of harpsichord composition peculiarly his own, there are many individual works by the composers mentioned above which are in no way inferior to those of the more famous Couperin. In some ways D'Anglebert and Louis Couperin went further than did François who, for example, left alone the so-called 'unmeasured preludes' which the two earlier men had developed, and which in the hands of a skilled performer can provide an unforgettable experience. We shall encounter wonderfully rich harmonies in François Couperin's music, yet there is no single page in all his works to match the incredibly bold dissonances found in the *Passacaille* of his uncle, Louis.

Couperin's luxuriantly embellished lyricism had its precedents in the suave melodies of Chambonnières, his seriousness and gravity in the suites of D'Anglebert, while his fondness for the picturesque stems from the Gallic tradition as a whole. Where Couperin stands above his predecessors and contemporaries is in the extraordinary variety of styles and techniques brought together in the four books, and in the sheer range of his musical imagination, fertilised by the French encounter with Italian music. He wrote 234 pieces, almost all of which are contained in his twenty-seven *Ordres*, spread over four books. (There are eight Preludes included with the publication of *L'Art de toucher le clavecin* (1716).) Book One, containing *Ordres* 1 to 5, appeared in 1713, and although the composer was by then forty-five years old and well known, it was his first real publication, for his two organ masses of 1692 had been issued by Ballard in manuscript copies only; his few engraved works were merely a handful of short songs scattered through some of the monthly issues of Ballard's *Recueils d'airs sérieux et à boire*. Book Two, containing *Ordres* 6 to 12, is undated, but evidence points to 1717 as being the likely year of publication. The two remaining books came out in 1722 (*Ordres* 13 to 19) and 1730 (*Ordres* 20 to 27). They cover a span of seventeen years.

Book Four was Couperin's last publication before his death in 1734 at the age of sixty-two, and its contents belie the composer's age and increasing ill-health. Although all the harpsichord pieces are, in a sense, the works of his maturity and advancing years, they seem rather to belong to that dream world for ever enshrined in the poetic image of the island of Cythera (birthplace of Venus, mother of Cupid) where youthful ardour and playfulness laughed at too serious a face. Yet while the prevailing mood is one of good humour and courtly grace, the dark shadows that sometimes fall over a page of Couperin's harpsichord music remind us that here is a reflection not just of an idealised world, but that of our own.

Whereas the German word *Klavier* (often spelt *Clavier*) was used as a generic term to include any stringed keyboard instrument (harpsichord, spinet, clavichord), the French words *clavecin* and *clavier* were specific. The former denoted the harpsichord, the latter the keyboard section (or manual) of that instrument. Even with its possibilities for tonal nuances, the clavichord was not popular with musicians in France who preferred the brilliance and richness of quill-plucked strings to the gentle and intimate murmurs of an instrument whose tone was produced by the key-lever itself pressing on the string, offering the performer direct control over the tone. On the other hand, the spinet, known in France as *épinette* and closely related to the harpsichord, was very common there; most works for keyboard by Couperin can be played on it. It differed from the harpsichord only by virtue of its shape, its strings running parallel to the keyboard instead of meeting it. Its restrictions were precisely those of a one-manual harpsichord, and therefore only those pieces which require two manuals (and these are very few) cannot be played on it. Although Couperin refers almost always to harpsichord, most of what he says is applicable also to spinet.

During the seventeenth and early eighteenth centuries French harpsichord makers were strongly influenced by the Antwerp workshop of the famous Ruckers family whose instruments were in constant demand in France, Germany and England. Their exceptionally good tone was so admired that when, in the eighteenth century, composers and performers began to demand a wider compass than available on these seventeenth-century models, many Ruckers harpsichords were reconstructed rather than abandoned; in fact few have survived in their original state. This process of reconstruction, known in France as *ravalement*, at the turn of the century so occupied the energies of the foremost French makers – such as the Blanchet family – that this has been advanced as the main reason why so few Blanchet harpsichords have been located.[1] Few French harpsichords from the seventeenth century have survived at all. Those that have are largely modelled on the Ruckers type with its sensitive action and brilliant yet rich tone. It would seem that at the turn of the century the French harpsichord in Couperin's youth was typically a two-manual instrument, the upper manual featuring an eight-foot register (i.e. its notes sounded at the pitch of the depressed keys), while the lower manual contained both an eight-foot and a four-foot register (i.e. the four-foot produced notes sounding an octave above the depressed keys). The two manuals could be coupled together by pulling the lower one out towards the player, thus engaging the mechanism. (There are a number of pieces by Couperin called *pièces-croisées* or 'cross hands' where the player is instructed to push back the lower manual.)

The compass of the French instrument at this time was nearly four and a half octaves from G (one and a half octaves below middle C) to C (three octaves above middle C). The lowest octave, as on

[1] Raymond Russell, *The Harpsichord and Clavichord* (London, 1959), p. 58.

most keyboard instruments before 1700, was a so-called 'short octave'. This arrangement took advantage of the fact that because so few composers of those days employed many chromatic notes in the lowest octave, the keys associated with these rarely used notes could be used for strings tuned below the lowest key provided on the instrument (in Couperin's youth usually B), thus extending the compass downwards without widening the construction of the keyboard. Other devices such as 'split keys', whereby the front section of a 'black' key played one note and the back section another, were also incorporated into the keyboard. Hence, although a harpsichord at the end of the seventeenth century might have B as its lowest *key*, the range of the instrument could be extended by tuning B down to G and 'splitting' keys C sharp and D sharp so that they sounded not only these notes but low A and B as well. The scale thus produced ran from G A B C C# D and chromatically up to high C. Harpsichords with solid C sharp and D sharp keys produced a scale G A B C D E F F# chromatically up to high C. During the eighteenth century *ravalement* was concerned very largely with reconstructing the keyboard to provide a full chromatic scale and to widen the range still further at either end. As far as tone and action were concerned the best earlier instruments were regarded as already having reached a state of perfection.

Although this final development in harpsichord construction was undoubtedly commencing in France in the early eighteenth century it is a fact that none of Couperin's works for the instrument include a low G sharp or C sharp. Low B flat is frequently found, but only in one piece (*Les Bandolines*, fifth *Ordre*) does this particular note share the music with a low B natural. It would seem that certain pieces by Couperin could be played on harpsichords with a 'short octave' only if the string were returned to B flat *or* B natural as the pieces required. That *Les Bandolines* was composed for the new harpsichords is also confirmed by the fact that in one bar Couperin calls for a low F (i.e. a tone below the seventeenth-century compass), and shown in the original publication as a lozenge-shaped note. It is curious that this extended range should be confined to one piece only, and that from the first book; for despite the fact that the last two books were published at a time when the move towards a wider compass was well under way, he never again required the low F. On the other hand, the later books reflect the trend towards providing additional notes at the higher end. In the first two books (1713,

1717) top C is the highest note. Having made tentative appearances in Book Three C sharp and D become quite common in the last (1730).

It was within these boundaries that Couperin moved with apparent freedom, his works for the instrument exploiting almost every technical possibility afforded by the harpsichord. Perhaps only Domenico Scarlatti went further in technical exuberance; typically Italian, however, Scarlatti did not explore to any great extent the rich field of keyboard ornamentation which is such a striking feature of the French *clavecin* school. Ornamentation as well as the programmatic nature of Couperin's pieces are the two features which first engage the listener's attention.

ORNAMENTATION

Like many others of the time Couperin regarded the harpsichord as a 'perfect' instrument – perfect in all but its incapacity to swell and diminish its tone through finger action. Yet even the absence of this aspect of musical expression can be largely overcome, he declared, through recourse to the fine art of ornamentation 'established by my predecessors and which I have tried to perfect' (preface to Book One). Thus the primary role of ornamentation in Couperin's harpsichord pieces, as in all his music, is an *expressive* one, a point easily overlooked if we think of it as a mere means of extending the evanescent tones of a plucked instrument. It is true that Couperin himself alludes to this additional usefulness of ornamentation when applied to the harpsichord. He pointed out in his *L'Apothéose de Lully* that anyone who wished to perform that work on two harpsichords instead of on strings and wind could do this effectively provided that the players extend the trills to the end of the note, for (as he says) the harpsichord is unable to sustain its tone for long. Nor can there be any doubt that some ornaments like the *pincé* (mordent) and the short fast trill can give a strong impression of dynamic accent to what is in reality a level tone. Yet to imagine that Couperin's rich ornamentation is there *primarily* to compensate for any deficiencies in harpsichord tone is to miss the point, and in doing so to ignore as well the equally rich ornamentation found in almost all his music.

As well as heightening the expressive qualities already present in the music (partly through those 'nuances of movement' described on pp. 21–2) the art of ornamentation in the French school added those little points of sparkling sound which one writer of the period, Michel Corrette, compared with the flashing fires of a polished diamond. Couperin gave a list of the embellishments he required, setting out their shorthand signs and their interpretation although, as mentioned earlier, he goes a little beyond these in the music itself.

Such ornaments were the common currency of European music during the eighteenth century, but the Italians tended to take ornamentation in another direction. As their fast (*Allegro*) movements left little opportunity for embellishment beyond the brittle mordent and the ringing cadential trill, it was to the slow (*Adagio*) movements that performers turned when wishing to exploit the art of ornamentation, especially in vocal music, sonatas and concertos. The 'gracing of the *adagio*' as it was called, while making use of the little embellishments and graces found in the French school went far beyond them, dissolving the slow melody into a rich display of passage-work involving scale- and arpeggio-type figuration, all of which (ideally) was improvised by the performer. (Quantz, Corelli, Handel and others have left written-out examples of the technique, making it possible to recreate the style in modern performances.) There is no evidence, however, to suggest that such a performance-practice was widely applied to Italian keyboard music, and as far as notation is concerned even the slowest harpsichord pieces by, say, Scarlatti contain very little ornamentation.

While the 'gracing of the *adagio*' was essentially an Italian (and hence German) practice the French went some way towards it in the *doubles* or *diminutions* of vocal music. As the art had also been cultivated by the seventeenth-century French lutenists who, as we shall see, exerted a strong influence on the French *clavecin* school, it comes as no surprise to find that Couperin provides florid alternatives for some of his harpsichord pieces, as for example in the well-known *Le Rossignol en amour* (*Ordre* 14). Our illustration (Ex. 25 overleaf) comes from the first *Ordre*.

If Italian ornamentation was very flamboyant and yet at the same time very restricted in its application (i.e. to the slow movements of ensemble music), that of the French was refined and ubiquitous. In most vocal and instrumental music in France the actual choice of ornament was largely left to the discretion of the performer (see p. 21). It was an art within an art; but it was also an art of improvisa-

Premier Courante, with 'double' (1st Ordre)

(a)

(b) Dessus plus Orné sans changer la Basse

tion. In contrast to this the ornamentation in Couperin's harpsichord music is calculated to the finest detail, little being left to
chance. We have seen how in order to ensure a correct performance,
the composer drew up a list of ornaments and their execution; his
L'Art de toucher le clavecin further demonstrated Couperin's inten-
tions by explaining his system of fingering, taking various difficul-
ties posed by certain passages in the *Ordres* and showing how to
overcome them. As far as the ornamentation was concerned Couperin's explanations were necessary not because his ornaments were
different from those in use (except perhaps the *aspiration* and *sus-
pension*) but because there was no universal agreement as to which
sign signified a particular ornament. D'Anglebert, for example,
employed a system of signs markedly different from those of
Couperin. Harpsichord composers generally preferred more specific indications than just the little cross which was found in vocal and
ensemble music, but their notation was a matter of individual
preference.

In the pursuit of calculated effects ornamentation in Couperin's
harpsichord music reached a new level of elaboration and difficulty,
and his keen displeasure with performers who, even after the
appearance of *L'Art de toucher le clavecin*, still played his music in
their own way is made very clear in the preface to Book Three.

I am always surprised to hear people who have learnt my pieces without
truly submitting themselves to my instructions. It is an unpardonable
negligence to place the ornaments arbitrarily how they wish. I declare that
my pieces must be performed in the way I have marked, and that they will
never make a true impression on people of real taste if one does not observe
to the letter all that I have indicated, neither more nor less.

Such are the demands posed by Couperin's ornamentation.

THE PICTORIAL AND PROGRAMMATIC ELEMENTS

Couperin's practice of giving fanciful titles to his harpsichord pieces
had its origins in the music of Chambonnières and the earliest works
of the French 'clavecinists' who, in turn, had borrowed the habit
from the lutenists of the late sixteenth century. Gaultier the Elder,
for example, liberally sprinkled his lute dances with titles such as
Courante des anges, *La Superbe*, *La Pleureuse* and so on, apparently also
establishing the tradition of giving a feminine form to the descrip-
tive word. Not all French harpsichordists, however, followed the

lead of the lutenists or of Chambonnières: D'Anglebert gave no such titles to any of the movements of his published suites, but this is not surprising, for his works, eschewing the 'fanciful', maintained a gravity that rather sets them apart. Even Chambonnières gave titles to only twenty out of his 150 or so pieces, and Louis Couperin to many fewer. Yet right from the start Couperin enjoyed adding picturesque names to various movements in his *Ordres*, and not unexpectedly this practice increased as he moved more and more into the genre of the 'character piece'.

Nevertheless we should not attach undue importance to a considerable number of the titles. It will be recalled that the composer himself had no hesitation in changing the original titles of his early trio sonatas when they were published many years later in *Les Nations*. A number of the harpsichord pieces were simply inscribed with the names of people associated with him in some way or another: *La Bersan, La Garnier, La Mesangère, La Gabrièle, La Nointèle, La Bontemps, La Conti, La Princesse Marie, La Villers, La Morinète, La Couperin, La Couperinette*, and so forth.[1] One imagines that these pieces caught something of the character of each person. Others are place names and nationalities: *La Charoloise, La Basque, La Castelane, La Boulonoise, La Verneuil*, etc. It is probably best to regard these titles as one does that of, say, Beethoven's 'Moonlight' Sonata: purely as a point of reference, a named piece being much easier to call to mind than one given merely a number, and this may well have been Couperin's intention here. On the other hand, there are also many other titles of a more pictorial or programmatic kind which provide a real clue to interpretation and appreciation. Yet whether truly programmatic or not, the very act of naming the pieces in the way he did betrays Couperin the Frenchman, the fanciful element in music traditionally having a strong appeal for the Gallic mind. 'Our music, whether it be for violin, harpsichord, viol or any other instrument, always seems to want to express some sentiment,' claimed Couperin, pointing to the way that French composers, unlike the Italians, even regarded metre and tempo in terms of *moods*, these being suggested by words like *vivement, tendrement* being placed at the head of French music (*L'Art de toucher le clavecin*).

The fanciful element is charmingly portrayed in those pieces by

[1] The meaning behind many of Couperin's titles is given in Jane Clark, 'Les Folies Françoises: Personalities in the music of François Couperin', *Early Music* (OUP), Vol. 8 no 2, April 1980.

Couperin which have a visual or onomatopoeic suggestion: *Papillons* (Butterflies), *Le Reveille-matin* (The Alarm Clock), *Le Carillon de Cythère* (Bells of Cythera), *Les Petits moulins à vent* (Little Windmills), *Les Tricoteuses* (The Knitters – finishing with the disaster of dropped stitches), to mention just a few. If the warbling of birds is sounded just once in the first *Ordre* (*Le Gazouillement*) it reappears in the fourteenth *Ordre* (*Le Rossignol en amour* and *Les Fauvettes plaintives*). The *Ordres* abound in scenes and portraits, subjects more elusive than those mentioned above but yet caught in a few deft strokes: *La Marche des Gris-vêtus* (March of the Grey-clad), *Les Bacchanales* (Bacchanalian Dances), *Les Vieux seigneurs* (Old Noblemen), *Les Jeunes seigneurs* (Young Noblemen), *La Mistérieuse* (The Mysterious One), *Les Ombres errantes* (Wandering Souls).

On a much larger canvas than those mentioned above is *Les Folies françoises, ou Les Dominos* from the thirteenth *Ordre*. The picturesque title alludes to the costumes (*dominos*) worn by guests at a masked ball. Each cloak and cowl is in a different colour and allegorises twelve virtues, qualities, temperaments or characters: Virginity (an invisible colour), Modesty (pink), Ardour (crimson), Hope (green), Faithfulness (blue), Perseverance (grey), Languor (purple), Coquetry (different colours), Aged Lovers and Retired Financiers (dark red and feuillemorte), Gentle Cuckoos (yellow), Taciturn Jealousy (dark grey), Despair (black).

Les Petits Ages (*Ordre* 7) is another series of portraits spread over various movements: *La Muse naissante*, *L'Enfantine*, *L'Adolescente*, *Les Délices*. It is not surprising that it is in the multi-movement works where we find the more truly programmatic pieces such as *La Triomphante* (*Ordre* 10) – a battle-piece evoking the sounds of war, joy of the victors and a fanfare – and, above all, *Les Fastes de la grande et ancienne Mxnxstrxndsx* (*Ordre* 11). This curious title refers to a powerful guild of Parisian instrumentalists which, in 1693 and 1707, had attempted to prevent Couperin and other harpsichordists from teaching their instrument unless they joined the *Ménestrandise* (hence, of course, Couperin's thinly-disguised title), by obtaining from it the licence of 'Master'. Couperin's appeals to Parliament succeeded on both occasions and he immortalised his victory in this satirical masterpiece. Its first 'act' is entitled *Les Notables et Jurés-Mxnxstrxndxurs* which, with its personalities and the solemn dignity of the music, could only refer to the legal court where Couperin's case was argued. Those who belong to the ancient guild are parodied mercilessly in the next three acts: hurdy-gurdy players, jugglers, tumblers and acrobats in the company of bears and monkeys. The infirm and the limbless, all still in the service of the guild, are caricatured in music of slow and jerky gait picturing the painful procession of dislocated legs and bent-over bodies.

Ex.26

Les Notables et Jures-Mxnxstrxndxurs (11th Ordre)

At last, all are put into total disarray by drunkards, bears and monkeys, the scene pictured in music of great brilliance and pictorial suggestion, even to the sound of the walking sticks (mentioned by Couperin in the score) heard tapping away as the invalid musicians hobble from the disorder.

Couperin returned only once more to the artifice of substituting x's for vowels in the title of a work: *Les Culbutes Jxcxbxnxs* (*Ordre* 19). Here, however, the significance of the title remains obscure, as it also does in one of the composer's best-known pieces, *Les Baricades mistérieuses* (*Ordre* 6). (Chambonnières also wrote a *Les Baricades* but it sheds no light on Couperin's.) There are a number of titles in the *Ordres* which are ambiguous or totally baffling to us nowadays. Even in their own day these same pieces might well have appeared enigmatic to all but a handful of the composer's circle. While their titles will no doubt always pique our curiosity, it would at the same time be a pity to imagine that Couperin's music depends for its effect upon the presence of non-musical elements. To be sure, in a good number of pieces they add an additional delight; but as in all fine music 'meaning' is revealed through the *musical* imagination of the composer – here in abundant evidence.

THE FORMS

Most of Couperin's harpsichord pieces are in two-part (AB) form with repeat signs placed at the ends of both sections. Sometimes the very last phrase of the piece is given an additional repetition at the reprise of B, and occasionally (as we have seen) Couperin provides optional florid versions for the repeats. This two-part structure dominates all but two of the named dance movements: allemande, courante, sarabande, gavotte, gigue, menuet, canaries, passepied, rigaudon, sicilienne (see Appendix C). While these dances make up at least half the movements in *Ordres* 1, 2, 3 and 8, the later ordres reveal a shift away from them towards more programmatic or 'character' pieces. Yet the spirit, if not the form, of the dance may not be far away, as in some of these later pieces like *La Régente; ou La Minerve* (*Ordre* 15), *La Superbe; ou La Forqueray* (17), *L'Audacieuse* (23), *La Convalescente* (26), which are, in reality, all allemandes. Nevertheless, there are also many movements which owe little to dance tradition. The trend away from dance forms can be seen as early as the fourth *Ordre* which contains no dances so-called (even though the final piece, *Le Reveille-matin*, is patently a gigue). It may well have been that Couperin envisaged right from the start that his collection of harpsichord pieces would go well beyond the mere sequence of dance forms implied by the term 'suite' (a word introduced into French keyboard music by Nicolas-Antoine Lebègue in 1687), preferring instead the term 'ordre' with its more widely embracing connotation of an 'ordered arrangement' of pieces.

Such an 'ordered arrangement' is achieved largely through the unity imposed by the key-schemes, each *Ordre* being in one particular key – both in its major and minor versions. (Thus C major and C minor regulate the third *Ordre*.) Only in the twenty-fifth *Ordre*,

also in C major/minor, is there a piece out of the prevailing tonality:
La Visionnaire, written in the relative key of E flat major, a procedure
which Couperin felt impelled to explain in the preface to Book Four.

It was mentioned that there are two dance movements not in the
sectionalised A B form; these are the chaconne and passacaille
(passacaglia). Believed to have originated as wild dances in Mexico
and Spain, they assumed a stately triple measure in the ballrooms of
seventeenth-century France and in the ballets and operas of that
country, their popularity lasting well into the second decade of the
eighteenth century. The words themselves had become synonym-
ous by the second half of the earlier century, so that it is not unusual
to find the same piece described as chaconne in one source and
passacaille in another; nor to find (as in *La Françoise* from *Les
Nations*) a movement described as 'chaconne ou passacaille'. No
amount of analytical ingenuity can unravel them. A distinction was
once made by Sébastien de Brossard in his *Dictionaire de musique*
(1704), who suggested that 'the passacaille was slower than the
chaconne, its melody more tender, its expression more heightened
and therefore almost always in the minor key'. While the comment
on tempo may have been correct (as far as dancing was concerned)
the rest is in no way borne out by the evidence of the many pieces
which have come down to us, either as dances or as instrumental
pieces. As far as French music is concerned, the terms must be
regarded as interchangeable.

What binds the chaconne and passacaille together is the invariable
presence of a recurring set of harmonies in cycles of four or eight
measures upon which variations (both melodic and harmonic) are
based. The characteristic harmonies found in these two forms, in
which one cycle flows into the next, spring from the stereotyped
basses, usually in a rising or falling scale (or part of it) often combined with leaps which establish clear tonality. If the bass pattern
recurs virtually unchanged the procedure is known as *basso ostinato*
or 'ground bass'. In practice, there are very few chaconnes or passa-
cailles in French music which employ a strict ground bass. Perhaps
the closest is a chaconne danced by Egyptians and Ethiopians in
Lully's opera *Phaeton*. Indeed there is only one example of a strict
ground bass in all the *Ordres – Les Folies françoises (Ordre* 13) – and
this is not a chaconne/passacaille dance-type. Characteristic of these
dances (which were usually performed at the conclusion of an act
in the *tragédie lyrique*) was that the music of each cycle should explore

new possibilities, unfolding and opening up new material in a ceaseless flow of melody and harmony. In chaconnes and passa-cailles composed for dancing it was most unusual for the music of previous cycles to be recalled. The style is magnificently caught in *L'Amphibie* (*Ordre* 24) described as '*Noblement, mouvement de Passacaille*'. One of Couperin's truly great works, it illustrates all the stylistic features of the form described above, except that the open-ing cycles are recalled at the conclusion. We quote the opening.

Ex.27

Noblement, mouvement de Passacaille L'Amphibie (24th Ordre)

If *L'Amphibie* closely resembles the form and style of those chaconnes and passacailles composed for dancing, it is not, how-ever, typical of the majority of French works which go by that name when written purely for instrumental performance, especially those for the harpsichord. From the time of Chambonnières on-wards composers from the French *clavecin* school were fond of grafting on to these yet another musical form: the rondeau (A B A C A etc.). Thus the majority of harpsichord pieces called chaconne or passacaille feature a refrain (*rondeau*) with intervening episodes (*couplets*), retaining at the same time those other features noted above. Couperin's Passacaille (*Ordre* 8) is in this more typical form of the 'rondeau passacaille', and this monumental and noble utterance (Ex. 28 overleaf) provides a worthy companion to *L'Amphibie*.

La Favorite (*Ordre* 3) is a 'rondeau chaconne', but this piece de-parts from tradition by being in quadruple instead of triple metre,

Ex.28

Passacaille (8th Ordre)

linked to the dance by virtue only of its grave and stately movement, and of course by its cyclic structure. At first sight the bass line seems to go beyond the stereotyped patterns typical of the chaconne and passacaille, but in fact Couperin has disguised through figuration what is simply a descending chromatic scale-segment common to countless *ostinato* types.

The ancient chaconnes and passacailles were often composed upon specific melodic formulae and their variants. These are repeated over and over in the bass, the stereotyped patterns being known by the names of the two dances. Another old dance often employing a characteristic bass melody was the romanesca, and although not so called, Couperin's *Les Baricades mistérieuses* is a kind of romanesca in that it takes up the old dance melody in the bass for much of the time. However, as in *La Favorite*, Couperin changes its metre from triple to quadruple and employs the rondeau form. *Les Baricades mistérieuses* is one of his finest rondeaux, the work unified by the ubiquitous presence of a single figure developed in masterly fashion throughout, in grand and sonorous expression.

Before leaving the cyclic-form pieces, mention must be made of *Les Folies françoises; ou, Les Dominos (Ordre* 13). We have already seen that the title refers to characters in a masked ball (p. 81), but its full significance is only revealed when the work is placed in relationship to a famous work by Corelli: the *La Follia* variations for violin and continuo. This is composed upon a recurring melody and bass known as *Les Folies d'Espagne* and, as Pierre Citron has shown, the extraordinary affinity between Corelli's work and *Les Folies françoises* leaves no doubt at all that Couperin was paying yet another tribute to the Italian musician whom he admired so greatly.[1] Although the two pieces have different basses and are in different keys (Corelli's being D minor, Couperin's being B minor), provided that adjustments are made to the accidentals the upper melody of *Les Folies françoises* can be played with *Les Folies d'Espagne*. Couperin's piece is the one example in the keyboard *Ordres* of a strict ground bass, each of the twelve movements representing one cycle of the long *basso ostinato*.

There are, in fact, only a few examples even of the 'free' cyclic forms in the *Ordres*. The great majority of pieces are in two-part (A B) form and the sectional rondeau (of which there are some forty examples). Couperin turned to the rondeau particularly for more extended music, although there are also a number of very short rondeaux, including some with only one *couplet*. The two-part and rondeau forms provide the structure for almost all the pieces, whether they be single movements or those comprising two or more movements. Thus, *La Triomphante (Ordre* 10) has three *parties*: *Bruit de guerre* (rondeau), *Allégresse des vainqueurs* (rondeau), Fanfare (AB). What is common to all the multi-movement works is that at least one *partie* is in the major or minor version of the prevailing key.

Couperin's structural schemes are thus very clear, but in two works he organises the form very ingeniously. *L'Epineuse (Ordre* 26) is a 'rondeau within a rondeau', the fourth *couplet* containing a second rondeau. Far more complex is *Les Gondoles de Délos (Ordre* 23) in which his two basic forms (rondeau and AB) are combined.

[1] Pierre Citron, 'Autour des Folies françaises', *Revue Musicale*, numéro spécial 226, 1955.

Some of the techniques of the French *clavecin* school had their roots in the music of seventeenth-century French lutenists whose *style brisé* (or 'broken style') considerably influenced the texture of keyboard writing. In this technique the notes of a chord are not all played simultaneously, but one after the other, as in the opening measures of a well-known piece *Le Tombeau de Mademoiselle Gaultier* by Denis Gaultier who cultivated the *style brisé* in his music for lute.

A sense of movement, lightness of touch, and a melodic line which, shared by more than one part, is woven into the arpeggiated texture are the chief features of the *style brisé* and it is easy to see how such a technique admirably suited the harpsichord, especially as the quickly fading sonorities of that instrument could be kept alive by the constant sounding of different notes of the chord. In contrast to the truly contrapuntal style evident in keyboard music based upon vocal or instrumental ensemble music, that which employs the *style brisé*, with its 'voices' which come and go, merely gives the *impression* of contrapuntal movement.

Traces of the *style brisé* are found throughout Couperin's harpsichord pieces, but in two of them (*Les Charmes* (*Ordre* 9) and *La Mesangère* (*Ordre* 10)) he actually describes them as '*luthé*'. When playing the first of these two pieces the harpsichordist is instructed to hold the notes so that the chords achieve full resonance – as on the lute where the strings freely vibrate until the next notes are plucked from them.

Ex.29

Les Charmes (9th Ordre)

The notation of the second piece more closely resembles the literal transcription of lute tablature.

Ex.30   La Mezangère (10th Ordre)

Not surprisingly, it is the *style brisé* that dominates a piece from the twenty-first *Ordre*, described by Couperin as being '*dans le goût de la harpe*'.

In works like *Les Baricades mistérieuses* (*Ordre* 6) (Ex. 31 overleaf), *Les Ombres errantes* (25) and *Les Idées heureuses* (2), to mention but a few, Couperin employs the *brisé* technique to produce passages of eloquent dissonance, as each group of held notes becomes blurred against the others in ever-shifting harmony. He takes the technique perhaps to its ultimate in *Les Tours de passe-passe* (*Ordre* 22), in which the melody so often is shaped by notes played by the left hand crossing over the right, its visual effect giving meaning to an otherwise enigmatic title.

Only one other piece was written for 'cross-hands' on one manual. This was *La Sézile* (*Ordre* 20), described as a *pièce croisé sur le grand clavier* – terminology which, in the light of five other works in the collection, is rather confusing. Each of these five (*Les Bagatelles* (*Ordre* 10), *Le Tic-toc-choc; ou Les Maillotins* (18), *Le Dodo: ou L'Amour au berceau* (15) and two *Menuets croisés* (22)) is also called *pièce croisé*, but was in fact composed to be played on *two* manuals, for the two hands pass in and out of the same register and

Ex.31

Les Baricades mistérieuses (6th Ordre)

so would collide on one manual. Yet, always the realist, Couperin suggested to those performers not possessing the larger instrument that they could still play these works if they transposed the right or left hand up or down an octave. Furthermore, he recommended these pieces to players of the viol, the violin or the flute for duet performance, provided – in the case of the flute – that the flautist taking the lower part adjusts the notes up an octave when they go out of range at the cadences.

Duet performance on the harpsichord is not neglected either: in *La Juillet* (*Ordre* 14), *Musette de Choisi* (15), *Musette de Taverni* (15) and *La Létiville* (16). Each being set out on three staves of music, they can be played either on two harpsichords (the bass line being duplicated) or on a two-manual harpsichord, in which case one player takes the top line of music only. Obiigingly, Couperin has written these pieces in such a way that the middle line may be omitted, thus making these pieces also available for solo performance! On the other hand, the *Allemande à deux clavecins* (*Ordre* 9) presumes the full resources of two players and two harpsichords who together produce a work of rich sonority.

If some of Couperin's harpsichord pieces are suitable for performance on flutes, viols and other instruments, there are others of course which are so bound up with keyboard techniques that they are virtually untranslatable. Such a work is *Le Reveille-matin* (*Ordre* 4) in which the sweet sleep suggested by the opening melody is constantly disturbed by the rude janglings of the alarm clock.

On many occasions Couperin explores the sombre tones of the harpsichord's lower register, an impressive yet clear sonority that can in no way be matched by the piano which tends to make works like *Les Sylvains* (*Ordre* 1) – notated entirely in the bass clef – sound rather lack-lustre. In other works it is the brilliant high register with which Couperin makes great play.

Although the composer suggested that many of these pieces could be played by other instruments, the impression persists – despite masterworks like *L'Apothéose de Lully* and others written for orchestral ensembles – that it was the harpsichord which was Couperin's 'natural' instrument, and one which drew from him his most personal music.

His lyrical genius found many an outlet in the *Ordres* for harpsichord, from the tuneful simplicity of the well-known *Soeur Monique* (*Ordre* 18) to the noble utterance of *La Raphaèle* (*Ordre* 8); and while it would be idle to deny that much of Couperin's lyricism is couched in the elegant and urbane language of French court music, there are works like *La Superbe; ou La Forqueray* (*Ordre* 17) which, in the gradual unfolding of long phrases and in the loftiness of thought, can be compared only with the music of J. S. Bach. There are some technical reasons also why *La Superbe; ou La Forqueray* recalls the style of Bach. They are concerned with the processes of motivic development on which so much German and Italian music is based. It can be seen also in these measures from Couperin's piece (Ex. 32 overleaf). It will be noted that these particular measures display no ornamentation whatsoever, strengthening further the impression that Couperin has for a moment moved away from the French style. It is something which can be seen in some of the earliest as well as the latest *Ordres*, and first encountered in *La Diane* (*Ordre* 2) in which the

Ex.32   La Superbe ou La Forqueray (17th Ordre)

hunting calls of the Goddess of the Chase are woven into the thematic material. Characteristic of the style, with its small amount of ornamentation, are running passages shared by both hands, often in imitation. Clearly reflecting the influence of the Italian keyboard sonata, it is illustrated in *La Diligente* (*Ordre* 2), *La Lutine* (3), *Fureurs bachiques* (4), *L'Etincelante ou La Bontemps* (11), *L'Atalante* (12), *Le Turbulent* (18), *La Couperin* (21), *La Bondissante* (21), and *Saillie* (27). With *La Bersan* (*Ordre* 6) Couperin goes further afield than the others in highly-wrought imitation and closely-knit texture. One of his finest works, it is the kind of music that Bach (or Bonporti from whom he may have borrowed the term) might have called an 'invention'.

And Couperin's harmony? At the height of the controversies which raged in Paris at the end of the seventeenth century over the virtues or vices of French or Italian music, champions of the foreign style were fond of comparing the harmonic daring of the Italian with the 'timidity' of the French. As mentioned earlier, it was largely as a result of Italian influence that French composers began to explore the wider implications of tonality and the expressive possibilities of rich harmony. It is true that in the pages of some seventeenth-century composers – Charpentier, for example, whose *Lamentations of Jeremiah* were mentioned on p. 36 – can be found passages of remarkably original, dissonant harmony, but these were the exception, not the rule, and in any case were bypaths in the development of European tonality – fascinating in themselves, but in no way affecting the course of the mainstream of baroque harmony. As Couperin once wrote, 'I love much better the things which touch me than those which surprise me', we should not expect to find 'daring' harmonies in his music. It is more in their sense of tonal 'stability' that they show how the composer absorbed the harmonic techniques of the Italians. Yet in his harpsichord music we constantly come across little 'brushstrokes' of harmony which add fascinating colours to the music, many of which would probably never have occurred to an Italian composer whose cast of mind tended to think in terms of modulation or key-change if striking effects were required. Here is a passage from the well-named *La Mistérieuse* (*Ordre* 25) in which the key of A minor is ruffled yet not shaken by the very curious appearances of B flat in the right hand, and the simultaneous use of D natural and D sharp in the next measure.

Ex.33   La Mistérieuse (25th Ordre)

To ears attuned to the style, these are fascinating little touches, and all the more effective because they are not over-done. The harpsichord pieces as a whole provide a never-ending source of fascination, as much in their imaginative strokes as in the sheer range of musical experience they convey. Yet, even more than this, his music embraces the human condition from its joys and humour to its sorrows. If it is expressed in a language of infinite refinement, we are the better for it.

Appendix A

Extracts from Chapter 6, *Of organists and organs*, of *The Paris Ceremonial, for the use of all collegiate, parish and other churches of the city and diocese of Paris*, by Martin Sonnet, priest, Paris, 1662, pp. 534–9

WHEN THE ORGAN IS TO BE PLAYED

11. At Mass it is played at the *Kyrie eleison*; at the *Gloria in excelsis*; at the repetition of the *Alleluia* with its neum, and at the last neum of the *Alleluia* before the gospel; at the sequence; at the offertory as far as the preface, unless a homily is given at that time or an announcement made, in which case the playing of the organ would cease and resume afterwards up to the preface; at the *Sanctus* and at the *Benedictus*, after the elevation of the Blessed Sacrament, up to the Lord's prayer; at the *Agnus Dei*; and at the *Deo gratias* after the *Ite missa est*. . . . It is not played at the *Credo*, but this is to be chanted.

WHEN THE NOTES OF THE PLAINSONG ARE TO BE PLAYED

16. The plainsong is to be played by the organ during certain prayers both at Mass and the hours to guide the celebrant, the singers and other officiants and the whole choir during the sacred liturgy and to give the correct pitch to the singers, lest cacophony and dissonance of voices result from its omission.

17. Therefore at Mass the plainsong is played at the first and the last *Kyrie eleison*; at *Et in terra pax* etc.; at *Suscipe deprecationem nostram*; at *In gloria Dei Patris. Amen*; at the sequence; at the first *Sanctus*; at the *Agnus Dei*; and at the *Domine salvum fac regem*.

WHEN THE ORGAN IS TO BE PLAYED EXPRESSIVELY,
SERIOUSLY, SMOOTHLY, SWEETLY AND HARMONIOUSLY,
IN ORDER TO MOVE CLERGY AND PEOPLE TO GREATER
DEVOTION

22. At Mass, at *Suscipe deprecationem* and at *Tu solus altissimus Iesu Christe*; at the solemn verse of sequences in which an invocation is made, whether this be sung three times or only once; . . . after the elevation of the Blessed Sacrament; and also while Holy Communion is being administered.

Appendix B

TEXT AND TRANSLATION OF THE LESSONS FROM THE
FIRST NOCTURN OF MATINS FOR MAUNDY THURSDAY

Lesson 1

Incipit Lamentatio Jeremiae Prophetae
(Here begins the Lamentation of Jeremiah the Prophet)

Aleph
Quomodo sedet sola civitas plena populo? Facta est quasi vidua, Domina gentium: princeps provinciarum facta est sub tributo.
(How is it that the city that was full of people now sits alone? How like a widow has she become, she that was great among the nations! She that was a princess among the cities has become a vassal.)

Beth
Plorans ploravit in nocte, et lachrymae ejus in maxillis ejus: non est qui consoletur eam ex omnibus charis ejus. Omnes amici ejus spreverunt eam, et facti sunt ei inimici.
(She weeps bitterly in the night, tears on her cheeks; among all her lovers she has none to comfort her; all her friends have dealt treacherously with her, they have become her enemies.)

Gimel
Migravit Juda propter afflictionem et multitudinem servitutis: habitavit inter gentes, nec invenit requiem: omnes persecutores ejus apprehenderunt eam inter angustias.
(Judah has gone into exile because of affliction and hard servitude; she has dwelt now among the nations, but has found no resting

place; her pursuers have all overtaken her in the midst of her distress.)

Daleth

Viae Sion lugent, eo quod non sint qui veniant ad solemnitatem: omnes portae ejus destructae, sacerdotes ejus gementes, virgines ejus squalidae, et ipsa oppressa amaritudine.

(The roads to Zion mourn, for none come to the appointed feasts; all her gates are destroyed, her priests groan; her maidens are filthy and she herself suffers bitterly.)

He

Facti sunt hostes ejus in capite, inimici ejus locupletati sunt; quia Dominus locutus est super eam propter multitudinem iniquitatum ejus: parvuli ejus ducti sunt in captivitatem, ante faciem tribulantis. (Her foes have become the head, her enemies prosper, because the Lord has made her suffer for the multitude of her transgressions; her children have been led away, captives before the foe.)

Jerusalem, convertere ad Dominum Deum tuum.
(Jerusalem, turn to the Lord thy God)

[Responsory (In monte Oliveti . . .)]

Lesson 2

Vau

Et egressus est a filia Sion omnis decor ejus: facti sunt principes ejus velut arietes non invenientes pascua: et abierunt absque fortitudine ante faciem subsequentis.

(From the daughter of Zion has departed all her majesty. Her princes have become like rams that find no pasture; they fled without strength before the pursuer.)

Zain

Recordata est Jerusalem dierum afflictionis suae et praevaricationis, omnium desiderabilium suorum, quae habuerat a diebus antiquis, cum caderet populus ejus in manu hostili, et non esset auxiliator: viderunt eam hostes, et deriserunt sabbata ejus.

(Jerusalem remembered in the days of her affliction and bitterness all the precious things that were hers from days of old, when her people were falling into the hand of the foe, and there were none to help her. The foe saw her and mocked her Sabbath observances.)

Heth

Peccatum peccavit Jerusalem, propterea instabilis facta est: omnes, qui glorificabant eam, spreverunt illam, quia viderunt ignominiam ejus: ipsa autem gemens conversa est retrorsum.

(Jerusalem sinned grievously, therefore she became filthy; all who honoured her despised her, for they saw her nakedness; yea, she herself has groaned and turned her face away.)

Teth

Sordes ejus in pedibus ejus, nec recordata est finis sui: deposita est vehementer, non habens consolatorem: vide, Domine, afflictionem meam, quoniam erectus est inimicus.

(Her uncleanness was in her skirts, she took no thought of her doom; her fall is terrible, she has no comforter. 'O Lord, behold my affliction, for the enemy has triumphed.')

Jerusalem, convertere ad Dominum Deum tuum.
(Jerusalem, turn to the Lord thy God.)

[*Responsory* (Tristis est anima mea . . .)]

Lesson 3

Jod

Manum suam misit hostis ad omnia desiderabilia ejus: quia vidit gentes ingressas sanctuarium suum, de quibus praeceperas ne intrarent in ecclesiam tuam.

(The enemy has stretched out his hands over all her precious things: yea, she has seen the nations invade her sanctuary, those whom thou didst forbid to enter thy congregation.)

Caph

Omnis populus ejus gemens, et quaerens panem: dederunt pretiosa quaeque pro cibo ad refocillandam animam. Vide, Domine, et considera, quoniam facta sum vilis.

(All her people groan as they search for bread; they trade their treasures for food to revive their strength. 'Look, O Lord, and behold, for I am despised.')

Lamed

O vos omnes, qui transitis per viam, attendite, et videte si est dolor sicut dolor meus: quoniam vindemiavit me, ut locutus est Dominus in die irae furoris sui.

(Is it nothing to you, all you who pass by? Look and see if there is

97

any sorrow like my sorrow which was brought upon me, which the Lord inflicted on the day of his fierce anger.)

Mem

De excelso misit ignem in ossibus meis, et erudivit me: expandit rete pedibus meis, convertit me retrorsum: posuit me desolatam, tota die moerore confectam.

(From on high he sent fire; into my bones he made it descend; he spread a net for my feet; he turned me back; he has left me stunned, faint all the day long.)

Nun

Vigilavit jugum iniquitatum mearum: in manu ejus convolutae sunt, et impositae collo meo: infirmata est virtus mea: dedit me Dominus in manu, de qua non potero surgere.

(My transgressions were bound into a yoke; by his hand they were fastened together; they were set upon my neck; he caused my strength to fail; the Lord gave me into the hand from which I cannot rise up.)

Jerusalem, convertere ad Dominum Deum tuum.
(Jerusalem, turn to the Lord thy God.)

Appendix C

DANCES OF THE FRENCH BAROQUE
(compiled by Margaret Mullins)

Allemande

Originated in Germany and was one of the oldest dances still performed at the Court of Louis XIV. Thoinot Arbeau, in his *Orchésographie* (1588), described it as a simple, rather sedate dance in duple time performed by several couples forming two lines. The allemande appeared in two forms in the early eighteenth-century ballroom – as a contredanse (for groups of four, six or eight dancers) and as a *danse à deux* (for one couple only). This last was certainly not sedate, as it was performed with many light springs and jumps which set the style of gaiety and grace. The particular manner of holding hands, where the arms were placed one behind the back, the other in front of the partner, was distinctive of the allemande. As the eighteenth century progressed, the manner of holding hands and interlacing arms became the all-important feature of this dance.

Bourrée

An *allegro* dance in duple time, originating as a peasant dance from Auvergne. Like the gavotte and rigaudon, it was adapted to the refinements of the seventeenth-century French Court and became a *danse à deux* of the ballroom and theatre. The principal step, the *pas de bourrée*, and other travelling steps alternated with jumps and hops in two-bar and four-bar dance phrases performed in a floor pattern based on the semi-circle and figure-of-eight. The simple structure of the social dance (two sections each of four, or a multiple of four bars, and beginning on a crotchet anacrusis) was more or less reiterated in theatrical bourrées, with occasional six-bar phrases occurring.

Canarie

Its origin is uncertain. It is believed to have come from the Canary Islands, though Arbeau offered the explanation that it originated in a Ballet or Mascarade in which the dancers were dressed as savages in feathers dyed many colours. He described it as a courtship dance in duple time in which the lady and gentleman advanced towards and retreated from each other, performing many difficult steps including *battements* (steps in which one leg is beaten against the other). Late seventeenth-century examples of the canarie are in compound duple time (6/4 or 6/8). It was a type of gigue danced to an air played quicker than that of the ordinary gigue. Examples extant in the dance notation of the period are technically very demanding, with *cabrioles* (a type of *battement* performed while in the air) and *pirouettes*, and are *Entrées* for productions of the court or theatre.

Chaconne

Appears to have had a varied career as early eighteenth-century descriptions range from a pantomimic dance enacted between Harlequin and Scaramouche to a Spanish court dance performed with castanets. The chaconne appeared in operas of the baroque period in two forms – as a rondeau and as variations on a ground bass. Examples in baroque dance notation are in the latter form and show the close relationship which existed between music and dance in France at that time.

Courante (French)

According to Pierre Rameau 'A very solemn dance' of the seventeenth century in triple time (generally 3/2). It was the first *danse à deux* performed after the branles (dances for the entire royal company) at the King's Ball. The courante contained no brilliant technical movements – no *battements* or *pirouettes* – yet was one of the most difficult dances to master, requiring great control and nobility of carriage. The principal step, the *temps de courante* or *pas grave*, set the restrained tempo and serious character of the whole. Although the courante was no longer in fashion at the turn of the century, it was still considered by the best dancing masters to be the basis of dance art and was made the centre of their teaching. The courante, sarabande espagnolle and English gigue were considered the link between social dance and the ballet as they rose above the simple practice of movement accompanying the musical beat as was seen for the most part in the ballroom. The music of the French courante was frequently characterised by shifts of metre between 3/2 and 6/4 (or 3/4 and 6/8), resulting in a fascinating rhythmic suppleness. This was in contrast to the music of the Italian corrente which was a dance in fast triple time.

Folie d'Espagne

Seems to have been not so much a dance with musical accompaniment as a particular musical composition in triple time with dance and castanet accompaniment, the dancer playing the castanets. The several examples from the period, described and notated, are all performed to the well-known melody of Corelli's *La Folia* variations. Descriptions of the *folie* range from suggestions for the inclusion of certain steps to notated virtuoso dances which include a great many ornaments such as *battements, ronds de jambes* and *pirouettes.*

Forlane

Said to have come from the Frioul in Italy whose inhabitants were called Forlans. In the seventeenth century it was very popular in Venice, especially amongst the gondoliers. There it was performed by one or two couples to a gay 6/8 rhythm, the dancers turning and leaping in a circle, sometimes with arms interlaced or passing overhead. The forlane was introduced to France in André Campra's *L'Europe Galante*, first performed in 1697. It was immediately popular, progressing in less than three years from a new form in the theatre to become a *danse à deux* in the ballroom. The French forlane was less vigorous than other dances in compound duple time. The more restrained tempo coupled with the uneven rhythm of its choreography gave it a hesitant, rather whimsical air.

Gavotte

Originally a peasant dance from the Lyonnais and Dauphiné. It was apparently accepted at Court in the second half of the sixteenth century as Arbeau apologised for the inadequacy of his descriptions, saying that the dance had not been in fashion in his youth. The gavotte as described by Arbeau was a collection of double branles intermingled with galliard movements, selected by musicians and arranged in a sequence. The dance was in duple time, normally in two parts although a third part was sometimes added – a musette of rustic character built upon a drone bass. The gavotte remained a group dance in the ballroom (though otherwise in the theatre) until the end of the seventeenth century. It followed the opening branle at the King's Grand Ball and was performed by the whole royal company led by the King and Queen.

Gigue

A somewhat tamer, English version of the Irish and Scottish gigue was introduced into France during the reign of Louis XIV. It is not known whether it was originally a group dance, though one example in the notation of the period, marked 'contredanse', suggests this possibility. The version of the gigue in compound duple time was known in France as the English gigue, thus distinguishing it from the gigue lente, a dance closely related in style to the loure, or Spanish gigue. This second version was a fairly slow dance which, although in 6/4, was danced as if in triple time, one bar of the music being equal to two of the dance.

Loure

Supposedly took its name from an ancient instrument similar to a musette. It was known as the Spanish gigue and, like the gigue lente, was an *andante* dance in 6/4 time. The very beautiful loure, *L'Aimable Vainqueur*, gained its particular musical quality from the *coupe de mouvement* (a step and spring) of which the dancing master, Pierre Rameau, wrote, 'they have been placed in the dance in different ways and so appropriately, that it seems that the leg expresses the notes.'

Menuet

First mentioned around 1664 and considered to be a descendant of the branle of Poitou. However, any similarity of the baroque social menuet to this branle as described by Arbeau is merely in the triple metre and gay tempo of the music. The former dance, though *allegro* in style, was performed with courtly restraint, while the branle was danced with jumping and stamping of feet. The seventeenth-century court menuet had for its main figure or floor pattern the S form so favoured by baroque artists. At the turn of the century this was modified to a Z figure which with the 'turn of the right hand', 'turn of the left hand' and 'turn of both hands' formed the figures for the dance. The French menuet was based on the *pas de menuet* (a series of four steps) which extended over two bars of triple time, these bars being divided into three equal parts; that is, while the music was in 3/4 the dance step was in 3/2. Musicians were advised not to stress the first beat of each second bar as it was confusing to the dancers.

Passacaille

According to one eighteenth-century source, passacaille meant vaudeville, the word coming from the Italian *passacaglia*. The passacaille of the French court was 'really a chaconne, the only difference being that the movement was more solemn, the melody more tender and the expression less lively' (Brossard, 1704). Examples of the dance in notation belong to the theatre. These show the choreography as visual representation of the musical form, variations on a ground bass.

Passepied

A choral dance from the north of Brittany and introduced to the French court in the second half of the sixteenth century, becoming a *danse à deux* which remained in the ballroom and theatre for almost two hundred years. The passepied was very similar to the menuet, the principal step being a variation of the *pas de menuet* performed likewise in a cross-rhythm. Thus the tempo was similar to that of the menuet though the time signature was 3/8 with the dance moving in 3/4.

Rigaudon

Came to the French court from Provence where it was a collective name for the folk dances of the region. The time of its adoption at court is uncertain, as the earliest extant descriptions date from 1700. These were *danses à deux*, similar to the bourrée except for the distinctive *pas de rigaudon*, an energetic kicking and jumping step. A type of theatrical rigaudon which had its origins in the *Commedia dell' Arte* existed at the same time. This was a buffon dance in which a woman belaboured a man with a broom, or two men kicked each other and hit each other with their hats. In another Harlequin was seen teasing a blind man who lashes out with his staff.

Sarabande

The gracious and graceful sarabande of Louis XIV's court had nothing at all in common with its supposed antecedent, the wild *zarabanda* of sixteenth-century Spain, which was described by a priest of the day as 'so indecent in its text, so repulsive in its movements, that even the most respectable people were inflamed by it' (quoted from Curt Sachs, *World History of Dance*, 1963). The sarabande, chaconne and folie came from the Spanish court to France. All three dances were danced with castanets, often to the sound of the guitar.

The sarabande, in 3/4 or 3/2, is neither as slow nor as solemn as the courante, as it contains fewer movements in the bar and in-includes some steps *en l'air*. A second version of the sarabande existed in the theatre. Known as the sarabande espagnolle, it was a dance in 6/4 time similar to the loure and gigue lente in that it was danced in simple triple, not compound duple time. The sarabande espagnolle, similar in dance style to the sarabande, cannot be confused with it. The musical rhythm of the former has a tie over the third and fourth crotchet beats in alternate bars and is generally in six-bar phrases, each phrase beginning on the second quaver of the fifth beat of the bar.

Sicilienne

Originally a folk dance from Italy, the eighteenth-century sicilienne was described as a gay dance in compound duple time with movements more strongly marked than those of the gigue. The exact manner of its performance in the court ballet is not known. Certainly it was considerably more restrained than the original, if musical examples are any guide.

Index of Works Discussed